travis michele gregory paul ali annen steven lucas maia jacob amy anne jomaura sean becka sasha suzannah david
lena dave kathy carolyn randy jason janet mark kent bruce cathy georgia warren andy alma jerry jamie drew alexis ed
ra paula karen beverlyjo ann ping bj sonja patty debbie carolyn michelle   is jimmy d
heather abigail matthew brianna brandon michael rachael jessica steph   lando cher
ard chester janey corrie mia aj naomi sheryl leon roseanne beverly jill l   nancy joy
jonathan cherise cornelia crystal lucia milly trasee lyndal hester sage m   elle tonya t
rayni olive karmen christina colleene mildred tresa luann mary jean ruthie hannah rachel irene kristen lynnda nozomi
a beckie adriana vera patti greg selby david rondi mary margaret mikaela cindi evy stacia leeanna allyson lori kristi n
le cynde glendene dorothy jocelyn regena betty sue pamela evaline carol anne ina lauriekay carmee lindis dirkje car
mari corrie fernande ricia janet laureen apryl brieanne earl kay lidia agnes rosanne krista diana-lee marvin joyce mar
jessica yvonne becky lorrie maureen mathew ilene sonia courtney bengt maryetta latrina miki marlin gayla jolene ro
ye mae crissy julie stacey lorett resa koeta myrna jeanna surma alanna gillian clela nadia dave mahala bente naomi
v nan madi lani mona melanie lola jodi reina marci danelle jessica wendy mary kelly velvet thelene fred april jacklyn l
ly nannette kathryn sherrill fiona maryann robert karan missy eve lee ann gretchen mariza marty karen heleen keri v
incent walleska bertha richelle erika sue ann bobbie bella phoebe simone cari leih jean ann ashley jeanie karma lill n
ni karen sue erica jacob kim tracie sheila serina l.marie kellie cheryll sharlene ceidys bj tella josie corie margo melody r
arisa bridget gunilla alyce julia jendra verla cecelia samantha saun berna shawn lorraine rose jessalcc daniclla alma
nie roger sophie elfi rosalinda roswita daphen frank siobhan alexis bonae susanne donnell catherine leeza donnamae
he dianna glenna tami sharilyn dayna clarice robie tiaann shirlee loretta cheryle liza ofelia clarissa twana dale carole de
lenese marsha rachael zabrina shantell ivette francine joe sharie angelica meline kelcy joni tomy lizette pattie kelie al
cheryls melissa ralph marge yaremis tim charleen danyelle lorene roseanna lavonne annette jo phylis katharine carin
elaine john michelle derba cherie christian lawrence betsey michael zandria lindee amam bonita debbie kaisa thelma c
mandy aileen twilah debora loraine tiffeni beth-ann cande barb darline angela maja kent susan blanca estela robyne l
la shanna charla cyndy aida marcy betsy gerry fahima dorothy ally maryelizabeth glenna serita autumn deana lena r
ee koren victoria corine geralynn jacquie nikki susy shawna terrilee hollie charlene jack robbie denyse niki madeline r
ll ambra galynn christene daveda marylin jeanette debe chasity pennie saundra alana corinne candace kami norma c
l lyn tracy james bernie rebekah dan rosalind jasmine michelle ludmila oliva bobbye brook floyce cristna debbi norine
elicia claire jimi sheryl jeannette marian malene pam inger ryan charles marilym stephanie wavel russell sue ellen ste
grace tricia mervin richard viki gearl donna jean alexandra rosalee georgia georgene jory mattie candy lois bernay ga
mae kenya dot dusan elizabeth marla seama brinda loeta jody alejandrina cary kari lynell daisy karlene nien cara sh
y aundrea grietje amandhalia jill lalysa hollis sharon gay-maree kaydra romona nelda olga leah betty ann tonda isab
die modesty allison irma janeen marcia arline gay norton herlide sandy logan mary lillianna nina heather timothy lin
y paulene cathie judith claudette tambry audrey laura lesley elisabeth sari sonya freddie audra mary jo pandy frances
a ben natalie geralyn letha tresia nona eddie roxane mary beth edith deena mayra patsy will jared raphael marcelle ma
a marilyn josephine valerie val karla kay terese channa delia marsue prudence francisca gale suzette larae constance c
n pearl ulla carla arlyce verma robbin aprille annette dean elin stefanie kathy rebecca lauren laurie janada marisol rika
carissa janice stacie liana melodie mary lou thea darla aysia amanda jim kc concepcion jen arleen lupe angelia anna-n
en charmaine brandon zelma shanda willie noelle jessi joey tony bettie theresa nellie lilly lisa ann shannon leona belle
ette yolie maribel henri kurt carolyn lydia joan miriam suzette jaime verna mark drusilla elsie cynthia phyllis vicky
claus laurel margaret lesley-ann mary ellen mollee deborah shannen bobbimaryfrances maedean irene silvia brandi e
machelle gwyn shana ghazala sherell cora renae ella viviann suzy kasey virginia lucille kate kyle mikel virpi alesia n
anne bonnie joseph lorie kathleen henrietta catrina eleanor robyn rev trish ivanna rae jeannie pikake passion liz kimb
n millie durecu bonny hetty kennith janis fran belinda margie suellen gayann leilani terry suanne jana katy kerry ha
erta ester sherrie anita rosemarie jo ann susana margret sam phil jayne latosha susannah kristy maura janel kesti haz
n ione abigail elly wynn nata maryjane wilma lovice karlie marita christee eilene gesela julianna mabel milady verlen
ylen annilu heartha marylou tina adele brigid sheli sue heidi gary selena dionne sophia reva trish janene tamela shelia
m merrill alan father mother peggy penny debra connie karen kesti amy marcia allen steve lisa karl heather abigail mat
ri tim tammy wendy justin bobby kylie kendall becky lisa bill sandra kate liz jason luke ann richard chester janey pa
nny wayne jay virl tom merrill alan father mother peggy penny debra connie karen kesti amy marcia allen steve lisa
bby kylie kendall becky lisa bill dotty mellissa chad haley harrison sandra kate liz jason luke ann richard chester janey
jonda fuzzy jolie regina jacque shari darlene bethania cathy cathleen lind kelly aundrea grietje amandhalia jill lalysa
helena roxanna elva ernestine mela mariana nora danna connie lesliann sandie modesty allison irma janeen marcia
gina brigitte patty scott esther stannah coby kaylene belva carolmarie misty paulene cathie judith claudette tambry
na cordelia kara lili delila benita micki jolea antoinette manette alessandra ben natalie geralyn letha tresia nona eddie

Fifteen Years of Friends

by
Marie Osmond

Foreword by Nayda Rondon
Editor, DOLLS Magazine

charisma
press

MARIE OSMOND
DOLLS
15th
"FRIENDS LIKE YOU"
ANNIVERSARY
1991-2006

First Edition
©2005 Marie, Inc.
Produced under license by Charisma Brands, LLC.
All Rights Reserved.
No part of the contents of this book may be reproduced without
written permission of the publisher.

ISBN 0-9773933-0-5

Editors Peggy Vicioso and Lisa Hatch
Art Direction/Design/Production bj Pergola

Marie Osmond's personal photos reprinted courtesy of Marie Osmond.

Printed and bound in China

Table of Contents

Olive May Osmond

As you can see from this photo, I don't remember a day in my life without a doll in it.

I learned how to love, laugh and nurture from my sweet mother who put a doll into my arms long before my feet took their first step.

After the many years in which my mother contributed dolls to my personal collection throughout my youth, it was such a joy to have shared my own doll line with her in her golden years.

Marie

Foreword

This is no diva;
she's as real & centered as they get.

You meet her and she instantly puts you at ease with her gregarious, funny and warm personality. It's no wonder her dolls are so appealing to so many. Each and every one comes from the heart of Marie and her team to touch a corresponding chord of emotion in her legions of fans and fellow collectors. Dolls are among Marie's most important bridges. They are her way of sharing her sentiments, hopes and good vibes with her fans. These admirers, in turn, thrive on this positive energy and pass it along to others they care about, and so "doll love" multiplies exponentially.

Both professionally as editor of DOLLS magazine and personally as an admirer of her many fine qualities, I've had the pleasure and good fortune to know Marie for several years now. I even had the distinct honor of chronicling her doll career in Marie Osmond's Collector Dolls, The First Ten Years (Portfolio Press, 2001). In the course of my research, I spoke with Marie and many of her colleagues, business associates, fans, family members and friends. I've also interviewed her several times for DOLLS and we frequently have featured her designs, including "Remember Me Rose," which graced our October, 2001 cover. I've gone to various doll events—from signings to collector club functions and Doll & Teddy Bear Expo appearances—where Marie was meeting her public and have seen first-hand her charisma and the great love her collectors have for her and her dolls, and how Marie returns it all with equal intensity.

Based on all these experiences, I've come away with a portrait of a wonderful human being, a passionate doll collector, and an inventive designer and sculptor who is constantly reaching for the next challenge. It's been so much fun to follow her progress and evolution in the doll world! Thanks to her open nature—and great stash of photos—we were able to get an insider's glimpse into her personal and doll world through the prior book, which covered her first decade of dolls. But now, in seemingly the blink of an eye, it's five years later. This time around she's decided to "fire" me (just kidding, Marie!) and write this second book herself—a move I wholeheartedly applaud. After all, what better person to get her feelings across than Marie herself! Marie has so much to say and it flows freely from her heart into her written words and doll designs.

During these last five years a lot has happened to her and those close to her. Not all of it has been good. Most notably, she lost her beloved mother. Deep loss has a way of putting everything else in our lives in a different perspective. For some it can crush us and deplete our souls. For others it can reinforce our essential beliefs and strengths. I'm firmly convinced that Marie belongs in the latter group. I sense that she's gone through deep spiritual and emotional trials and come out even more eager to give of herself and her talents.

I, for one, can't wait to see what she has to share with us this time around. So settle down in a cozy reading spot and get set to welcome Marie and her cast of doll characters into your home and heart.

Nayda

Me with Nayda Rondon,
Editor of DOLLS Magazine

I've been dipping

my clay covered fingers into a china

saucer from one of my mother's favorite collections. The delicate poinsettia pattern on the inside edge of the china has become coated with a gray-colored paste. I'm as happy as a preschooler making mud pies after a heavy rain, except I'm using my mom's best china in the process. Somewhere deep inside of me I know my mother would approve. She always thought that any time spent doing something creative was like a mini-holiday.

Earlier in the morning I had set up a doll sculpting area in my house, covering the carpeting, tabletops, walls and chairs with plastic sheeting, yards and yards of it. (Did I say yards???) One lesson I learned quickly, after the first time I ever sculpted, is this: the clay that is used to sculpt faces…really has legs! It can travel. Far! I've had a bagel come out of the toaster a week later with clay dust stuck to it.

I'm even considering leaving the plastic down permanently. With four children under age nine it would be a real time-saver when it comes to cleaning the house. You could just hose off the sheets of plastic. Good idea, right? I finally understand why my grandparents

Talk about having too much fun…we were! Lisa is sculpting "Little Red," Karen Seamons sculpted her granddaughter, I am sculpting "Friendship" rose, and Karen Scott is there to keep us all on track! (Good luck with that, Karen!)

covered any upholstered object in their house with plastic slipcovers. It wasn't a style choice. It was a mental health choice. There's no stress when you can just wipe off the couch after the grandkids come over.

My sculpting partners for the day arrived soon after: Karen Scott, a gifted sculptor who is giving me tips this week, Karen Seamons, seamstress extraordinaire, and Lisa Hatch, my Creative Director and the true sister I never had. We gathered in the foyer, putting on our full body aprons, near the 9-foot evergreen tree which graces the entryway year-round. Each branch is adorned with a Marie Osmond Tiny Tot doll (proof that we had sculpted before...and we will sculpt again!).

This is vintage Olive Osmond...with the grandkids gathered around, involving them in learning of some kind. This time it happens to be baking. (Watch out Mother, Jimmy is trying to sneak up and steal a cookie!)

We immediately prioritize our day by freeing the contents of a bag or two of chocolate candy, (Okay, five. Before lunch.) and get to work. All three of my sculpting partners nodded their heads in understanding when I brought to the table the saucers containing water-filled sponges that we would use to keep our fingers moist for molding the clay. They can appreciate that using my mother's china helps me to feel her presence while I sculpt a new doll for my line.

I trust my intuition

when choosing people to work with because it's important to me that we share more than the same vision; we share the same dedication to each other as good friends.

As it turns out, I've found dear, loyal friends who are not only brilliant in helping me create my doll line, each has a genuine enthusiasm for life and a compassionate heart. My gratitude for the wonderful friends I have in my life was the inspiration behind the 15th Anniversary theme of "Friends Like You." It is so significant to have true friends who can mutually celebrate each other's joys and support each other through the sorrows. And, on this day, as we sculpt, I know I am in the company of understanding friends.

Both Karen Scott and Lisa have recently lost their own mothers and as we create new faces for upcoming dolls, we all exchange stories of the women who shaped our lives so beautifully in the past.

As you may know,

my mother was my very first and best lifelong friend.

She was the one who started me on collecting dolls. I think she was so happy, after giving birth to seven boys in a row, to finally have a daughter to dress in pink and who could share her passion for the delicate beauty and character that dolls bring into your life. (Let's face it, after sharing a household with nine men, I think my mom and I would have collected anything that had it's mouth sealed shut!) But, my mother wasn't all that delicate with her collectibles. She believed that you should use and appreciate those things that bring you joy. It's the main reason I insist that the porcelain that I use in my doll line be able to hold up under regular living. When we were growing up, there were many, many meals shared on my mother's best china. It was her way of acknowledging and teaching us what was important: that possessions should always take second place to the people you love.

It was a labor of love for me to create "Olive May Loving Tribute" in honor of the best girlfriend and doll-collecting cohort a girl could ever have . . . my mother.

It was a lesson my mother learned at a young age from her own grandmother. She had passed along to me a story of when she was a little girl and she dropped and broke a china plate from her grandmother's collection. Frightened that she would be in trouble, my mother approached her grandmother in tears. She remembered distinctly the impression it left on her when her grandmother dried her tears and said:

toss out the plate, Olive, it's only sand.

Without a doubt, the china was beautifully refined sand, yet I feel that my great-grandmother was right. In its original form, every material possession in existence is just an element whose value is determined by the perspective of people. What matters most is the happiness, sense of comfort and warmth that it brings to someone. This became my highest hope and desire when I started my line of collectible dolls fifteen years ago. I wanted it to bring joy and a common bond to those who collect. The sense of accomplishment I value most comes from hearing from collectors about the great community and relationships that have developed because of the dolls. I always look forward to my doll signings at the great doll stores across the country or at Disneyland. Not only have I become close friends with the storeowners, I also cherish the friendships I have built over the years with my collectors. And, more than that, I'm so happy to hear about the friendships my collectors have found with each other. I love hearing of how mothers have a passion they can share with their daughters, sisters can collect from opposite sides of the country, and friendships have unfolded around the world with dolls as the starting dialogue.

My mother had a deep wisdom in having me collect dolls. She knew that there is a universal quality in dolls no matter what the language or the culture. Dolls have been treasured objects in the lives of people for as long as there have been children. They have been found in ancient Egyptian tombs that are three thousand years old. The desire of a child to take care of a doll, and of a parent to give a child a doll seems to have existed since the beginning. I would even venture to imagine that Mother Eve herself made her own little children some dolls out of the bounty of the earth, perhaps with pebbles or seeds of grain for eyes and golden flax or corn silk for hair. (Probably Eve's little daughters took a sharp stone to the corn silk hair and cut it all off into a crew cut, just like we did as preschoolers with some scissors on the locks of our first dolls. I think that's another trait that's been passed down throughout history, don't you?)

Here I am with a few of my closest friends! We did this center page photo shoot for the National Enquirer in November, 1993. In just two short years since starting my line of dolls, we had created over 150 dolls!

Dolls definitely reflect the social and cultural history of humanity. In fact, they are such a large part of our society that currently, on any given day, a search on ebay will yield over 80,000 items listed that contain the word "doll" in the description.

 I remember thinking to myself when I posed with "Remember Me" in 2001 for my 10th Anniversary book cover, that I couldn't believe it had been 10 years already. And now, 5 years . . . 13 rose dolls . . . countless doll friend memories . . . and many hairstyles later . . . here we are at our 15th Anniversary! Time seemingly stands still when you're "playing dolls!"

We doll collectors are a considerable and varied group of people.

I've had the pleasure of meeting so many collectors who have come to my doll signings and who have filled the audience seats at my QVC shows. Lisa and I were recently recalling our fun trips to retail stores, doll fairs and events, and to Disney for signings and she estimated that I've signed at least 18,000 dolls within the last five years. No wonder I can barely hold this sculpting tool I'm using to shape this cheekbone. It's like carpal tunnel claymation!

On a nearby shelf I've put my "Remember Me" Rose doll as a reminder to keep the faith in my pursuit of a fresh, new sculpt. She is the doll I sculpted for the debut of what has become our most popular series of dolls ever, the "Coming Up Roses" collection. Cultivating roses was another great passion my mother and I shared and I've come to realize that it's an interest shared by thousands everywhere.

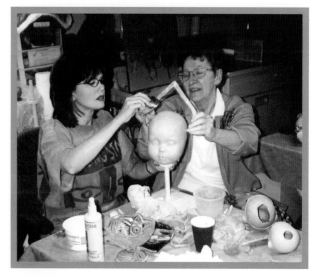

Sculptor Sonja Bryer and I having way too much fun while sculpting together in her studio. I was sculpting "Remember Me." Note that the doll's head is as big as mine!

"Remember Me" was also created to celebrate the ten year anniversary of Marie Osmond dolls. It's hard for me to believe that five years have passed since I sat in the basement workshop of another friend and talented sculptor, Sonja Bryer, and wondered (or, to be honest…panicked about) what look would emerge for this first rose doll. But, that wasn't the only thing I was contemplating that chilly week in Ohio, shortly before Thanksgiving.

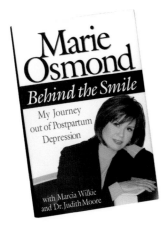

In 2001, I shared my own journey through PPD, and was amazed to discover how many others had been on the same path.

I was also finishing up my New York Times best-selling book "Behind the Smile" about my experience with postpartum depression. I had no idea what an overwhelming reaction the story of that struggle would bring from thousands of people across the country. Whether or not they had ever experienced depression, it seems obvious to me that many are feeling a compelling need to reconnect with matters of the heart: our faith, our families, our friends, and making our homes into a welcoming, safe harbor. This was especially illuminated for me as I recovered from PPD. I was a woman who was very successfully "doing" my life, but forgetting to "live" my life. I realized that I was no longer content to have my furniture be a suitcase and my zip code be a tour bus. Even though other television offers and Broadway show contracts were on the table, I knew that it was time to re-prioritize my life. The next week I celebrated Thanksgiving with my family, my husband, our children, and my sweet parents. I decided then and there that everything I truly treasured was gathered at that table. (No, I'm not talking about the turkey…though some of my brothers are turkeys…treasured turkeys nonetheless). Even after considering how much I enjoyed every curtain call and appreciated each credit roll of my public career, I knew I was missing the chance to make personal memories with my loved ones.

I'm so **grateful** I listened to my **heart** on that day,

because in less than one year, my sweet mother would have two major strokes, leaving her physically incapacitated for the remainder of her days. But, her spirit and wisdom as my greatest earthly teacher never left and I was blessed by spending countless hours with her in those last years.

I guess you could say my mother was an unrelenting stage mother, in the best way. She was there for me every single "stage" of my life. Through my childhood, my early show business years, each of my recordings, Broadway shows and television shows, my marriage and all eight of my children, my mother was there to acknowledge and support me in each new stage of my life. It was such a privilege for me to be

This was a common scene of my childhood - me by my mother's side as she tutored and trained me.

there for her in the final stage of her life. I took the time to do those things with my mother that we had always promised ourselves we would do once we weren't so busy. Since my mother wasn't able to keep as physically active and busy as she always was, we spent hours doing

Here I am with my sweet Daddy.

only those things that gave her such simple pleasure. I brought over fresh-picked cherries and she sat nearby in her wheel chair filling jars with fruit and we bottled enough to last a year! I set up her sewing machine next to her hospital bed and we had long talks about motherhood and spirituality as I stitched quilts. My mother

found the humor in the "designer" hospital gowns made especially for her out of fun, animated fabrics, like a cute Betty Boop print. I sat bedside with her in the hospital and knit scarves and hats. I jotted down her life advice and stories as she told them to me, so that even my youngest daughter (then only 14 months old) would be able to know her grandma. My father would come in and out of the room, bringing a pretty plant, a card from a fan, or just fluffing up the pillow for "his girl."

My parents
were best friends
throughout their marriage.

My mother took such joy in my doll line, and especially in her last year she loved to have a doll or two nearby her bed. While she was in the hospital, she had the little angel Tiny Tots perched on the window ledges. At home, she lined the tops of all of her cabinets with my dolls. In the kitchen, she had the entire Wizard of Oz collection peeking out from behind canisters and potted plants. Her love for this series could be encompassed in the motto she shared with the movie: "There's no place like home." In the most prominent place on the counter was her personal favorite, the Wicked Witch of the West. When I asked her about it, she said it reminded her to never have a melt down. It's not worth it. This is great generational advice that I pass along to my own daughters. (You may have noticed in the Oz collection that the witch is just slightly smaller than the others. I thought, maybe, she melted down just a bit.)

My mother also had two large glass curio cabinets filled with my dolls. Every year of my life she and I put a doll for each other under the Christmas tree. Even when she was unable to vocalize her thoughts, I could always tell when my mother loved a doll. Her eyes really lit up when I brought Baby Adora Belle into her room.

I think Adora Belle was a favorite of hers because she calls to mind Betty Boop's wide-eyed appeal.

One of my fondest childhood memories was waking up on Christmas morning to find a doll or two (or three, or four!) under the tree from my mother and "Santa". Even now, I still love finding a doll under my tree . . . as well as <u>on</u> my tree!

My mother had such a special connection to dolls that, following her passing, each of her daughter-in-laws (whom she always called her daughters) and granddaughters (okay, the grandsons too) asked to be given one of Mother's dolls as a keepsake. What a significant memory, to have a doll to hold, even after grandma had gone on to her eternal life. My brother Wayne's daughter, Sarah Elizabeth, is an RN who spent a significant amount of her time taking exceptional care of my mother, especially in her final year with us. My mother's comfort was her greatest concern. I decided Sarah should be given the original "Olive May" doll that held the place of honor in my mother's curio cabinet. She openly wept as I placed the doll in her arms. I hope some of the comfort she so freely gave to my mother will return to her each time she looks at her "Olive May" doll, knowing that her grandma was always grateful for such tender care.

As we were laying out photographs for this book, I could also attach a significant memory to each doll. But, my memories were of the support and love I have felt from my doll collectors over the last five years. I'll never forget the kindness of my doll friends who offered to give me their original dolls from their own collections after my house fire damaged and destroyed some of my dolls.

I met Emmerson Rose at a Disneyland signing, and she was a real "personality" as you can easily see from this photo. She knew her dolls too! She became the inspiration for the "Emmerson Rose" doll, from our "Portrait" series, and was sculpted by Sonja Bryer.

It's been **proven** to me over and over that doll collectors are the most generous,

good-hearted, loyal, extended family for which anyone could ask. I constantly hear inspiring stories of doll collectors uniting to assist a fellow collector who is experiencing a difficult situation. I was witness to your generosity when Lisa's sister, M'Lissa, lost her husband to workplace violence. Your selfless concern and support for each other is apparent when I read the posts on the Marie Doll Friends forum. Every hug and card and, yes…every bag of chocolate…you have given me in the last five years has strengthened my spirit (even if it did weaken my knees from carrying the extra weight I put on!). But, you have also been there to celebrate the victories: the DOTY awards for "Young Love," "Marie," and "Little Miss Muffet," as well as the nominations, having the "Olive May Loving Tribute" doll and our new "Babies-a-Bloom" find their place in history as the "Top 10 Hot Collector Dolls of 2004." And, as far as I'm concerned, I believe that going together through whatever trial or treat life may bring, is the true definition of family.

I'm blessed to have "friends like you."

The reasons we collect dolls are probably as varied as doll collectors. Some of us may have had wonderful childhoods that we wish to remember and some of us may have had lonely or harsh childhoods and collecting dolls is a way to perhaps capture those moments we never had. Some may see it as a fun pastime, and others as a passion. But, I do know that doll collectors understand the heart of it all.

No matter what circumstances may affect our lives on any given day, there is a sweet reminder of the goodness of life in the sparkle in a doll's eyes, the beauty of the fabrics for their outfits, the charm of an expression that is captured in their faces.

It's important to me that Marie Osmond Dolls are not only visually appealing, but that they also evoke an emotional reaction. It's been studied and proven that our best memories have a strong emotion attached to them. I know that a doll can bring to the surface a long-forgotten experience, a moment of simple joy, a sentimental feeling, or a reminiscence of a time gone by.

A **doll** should be that gentle reminder to stop "doing" life and start "living" it.

In the same way that I took interest in my mother's passion for dolls, I've enjoyed watching the collector's flame being ignited in my own children. My second oldest daughter has a great sense of style and keeps her eyes on the trends for me. She informed me a while back that when she is eighteen years old she will be ready to take over my doll line because, as she told me: "You will be way too old to work." Don't you just love kids? One evening, I came home to find her watching a collectible bear show. She was taking notes on their accessories and gave me her opinion. "Mom," she said. "One of the bears was wearing a bear fur coat. Don't you think that's gross! I mean, that would be like you wearing Uncle Donny." I told her: "I would never wear Uncle Donny. I don't like polyester. (smiles)" At least she's observant. But, then, aren't all true doll collectors?

Whether you have one doll or one thousand,

I hope you collect Marie Osmond Dolls because you can count on my dedication to quality and ferocious attention to the details. I want each doll to be something you can look forward to displaying in your home, giving as a gift, or passing along to those you love as a keepsake. I appreciate both your confidence and your loyalty. I am so pleased to present this book to you, my friend, not only as a photographic journal of the last five years, but as a commemoration to whomever that first person was to place a doll in your hands and ignite a passion for collecting in your heart. In the same way that I know my mother is pleased that I find happiness, connection and warmth in using her good china, I am delighted that you enjoy Marie Osmond Dolls.

Marie

2000 - 2006

a

Coming Up *Roses*

Roses are one of life's most perfect pleasures, blossoming in splendor and awe, right before our eyes. Each one is unique, yet perfect in its own way. This was the inspiration for my "Coming Up Roses" collection. Like a rose, each of these dolls is unique, yet perfect, with a few unexpected surprises such as a dozen trim roses embedded within the dress design and an accompanying collector pin.

b

c

a. Remember Me, 2001, *Sculpted by Marie Osmond, Edition 20,000*
b. American Classic, 2001, *Sculpted by Sonja Bryer, Edition 3,000*
c. Peace, 2001, *Sculpted by Sonja Bryer, Edition 3,000*

a. Queen Elizabeth, 2002, *Sculpted by Sonja Bryer, Edition 20,000*

b. Princess, 2002, *Sculpted by Sonja Bryer, Edition 7,500*

c. Child's Play, 2003, *Sculpted by Karen Scott, Edition 7,500*

d. Young Love, 2003, *Sculpted by Emily Garthright, Edition 15,000*
e. Yellow Rose of Texas, 2004, *Sculpted by Beverly Stoehr, Edition 3,000*
f. Heaven On Earth, 2004, *Sculpted by Sonja Bryer, Edition 3,000*

a. White Christmas, 2004, *Sculpted by Karen Seamons, Edition 3,000*

b. Baby Darling, 2004, *Sculpted by Lisa Hatch, Edition 3,000*

c. Marie, 2005, *Sculpted by Emily Garthright, Edition 17,500*

d. Friendship, 2006, *Sculpted by Marie Osmond, Edition 17,500*

d

Rose Bud

I am very pleased to present my "Rose Bud" collection, which are miniaturized replicas of the dolls from my "Coming Up Roses" series, offering proof positive that good things _do_ come in small packages!

a

b

c

d

e

f

g

h

i

j

k

l

a. Remember Me Rose Bud, 2003, *Sculpted by Marie Osmond, Open Edition*

b. American Classic Rose Bud, 2003, *Sculpted by Sonja Bryer, Open Edition*

c. Peace Rose Bud, 2004, *Sculpted by Sonja Bryer, Open Edition*

d. Princess Rose Bud, 2004, *Sculpted by Sonja Bryer, Open Edition*

e. Queen Elizabeth Rose Bud, 2004, *Sculpted by Sonja Bryer, Open Edition*

f. Child's Play Rose Bud, 2004, *Sculpted by Karen Scott, Open Edition*

g. Young Love Rose Bud, 2005, *Sculpted by Emily Garthright, Open Edition*

h. Yellow Rose of Texas Rose Bud, 2005, *Sculpted by Beverly Stoehr, Open Edition*

i. Heaven on Earth Rose Bud, 2005, *Sculpted by Sonja Bryer, Open Edition*

j. Baby Darling Rose Bud, 2005, *Sculpted by Lisa Hatch, Open Edition*

k. White Christmas Rose Bud, 2005, *Sculpted by Karen Seamons, Open Edition*

l. Marie Rose Bud, 2005, *Sculpted by Emily Garthright, Open Edition*

Material Girls

I remember my mother exclaiming, "She who dies with the most fabric... wins!" Call it "materialistic" if you will, but I think she was on to something! (smiles) My "Material Girls" are fabric friends who are fashioned for fun, and just like our own friends, each fabric is distinctly unique. Each brings a different look, feel, texture and design to enrich and beautify our lives.

a. Velvet, *2005, Sculpted by Karen Scott, Edition 3,000*

b. Nettie, *2005, Sculpted by Karen Scott, Edition 1,500*

c. Cotton Ginny, *2006, Sculpted by Karen Scott, Edition 3,000*

d. Satin, *2005, Sculpted by Karen Scott, Edition 1,500*

e. Lacey, *2005, Sculpted by Karen Scott, Edition 1,500*

f. Chenille, *2004, Sculpted by Karen Scott, Edition 3,000*

c

d

e

f

a

Collectibles

This series of beautiful dolls, in my opinion, represents the "Classic" dolls of the future. In every way, these dolls define collectibility.

a. Sabrina, *2005, Sculpted by Karen Scott, Edition 2,000*

b. Tabitha, *2003, Sculpted by Karen Scott, Edition 2,000*

c. Arabella, *2004, Sculpted by Karen Scott, Edition 750*

d. Breena, *2005, Sculpted by Karen Scott, Edition 2,000*

a

b

c

d

a. Brynn, 2003, *Sculpted by Kathy Smith-Fitzpatrick, Edition 1,500*

b. Kesti 2002, 2002, *Sculpted by Joke Grobben, Edition 2,500*

c. Penelope, 2001, *Sculpted by Penelope Carr, Edition 1,500*

d. Shelley, 2002, *Sculpted by Kathy Smith-Fitzpatrick, Edition 2,000*

Not shown Brynn Springtime, 2005, Sculpted by Kathy Smith-Fitzpatrick, Edition 50

e

f

g

h

i

e. Budding Virtuoso, 2003, *Sculpted by Karen Scott, Edition 1,000*

f. 15th Anniversary Bunny Love, 2005, *Reproduction Bunny Love Sculpt, Edition 1,500*

g. Bunny Love Anniversary, 2001, *Reproduction Bunny Love Sculpt, Edition 5,000*

h. Victorian Bunny Love, 2004, *Reproduction Bunny Love Sculpt, Edition 1,500*

i. Victorian Christmas Bunny Love, 2004, *Reproduction Bunny Love Sculpt, Edition 2,000*

a. Tea For Two, 2002, *Sculpted by Kathy Smith-Fitzpatrick, Edition 2,002*
b. Babette, 2005, *Sculpted by Karen Scott, Edition 250*
c. Rosemary, 2001, *Sculpted by Jessica Antoinette, Edition 991*
d. Sunday Stroll, 2003, *Sculpted by Jessica Antoinette, Edition 1,500*
e. Stella, 2004, *Sculpted by Karen Scott, Edition 250*
f. Rae, 2002, *Sculpted by Karen Scott, Edition 1,500*

d

e

f

46

a. Mary, *2005, Sculpted by Karen Scott, Edition 300*
b. Vivian, *2004, Sculpted by Sonja Bryer, Edition 750*
c. Tessa, *2002, Sculpted by Marguerite Shirley, Edition 2,500*
d. Starry, Starry Night, *2004, Sculpted by Sonja Bryer, Edition 750*

a

b

c

d

Heaven's
Helpers

I believe in angels! I know that whether we recognize it or not, we all receive a little help from Heaven now and then.

a. Snip'n Snowflakes, *2005, Sculpted by Jo Ann Pohlman, Edition 3,000*
b. Rain Dropper, *2006, Sculpted by Jo Ann Pohlman, Edition 3,000*
c. Star Twinkler, *2005, Sculpted by Jo Ann Pohlman, Edition 3,000*
d. Cupid's Helper, *2005, Sculpted by Jo Ann Pohlman, Edition 3,000*

San Francisco *Music Box Co.*

a

b

c

a. Enchantment, 2002, *Sculpted by Michael Evert, Open Edition*

b. Timeless, 2002, *Sculpted by Michael Evert, Open Edition*

c. Perfection, 2002, *Sculpted by Michael Evert, Open Edition*

d. Veronica Violet, 2001, *Sculpted by Adrienne Brown, Edition 2,500*

d

Sweet Sachet

Home Decor

Pin cushion dolls date back to the 1800's, and were originally designed to be more functional than displayable. My, how times have changed!

a

b

c

d

e

f

a. On Pins and Needles, 2001, *Sculpted by Michael Evert, Open Edition*

b. Cinderella, 2006, *Sculpted by Michael Evert, Edition 500*

c. Apricot Nectar, 2004, *Sculpted by Michael Evert, Open Edition*

d. Lavender Lady, 2004, *Sculpted by Michael Evert, Open Edition*

e. White Angel, 2003, *Sculpted by Michael Evert, Open Edition*

f. Pink Ruffles, 2004, *Sculpted by Michael Evert, Open Edition*

g. Red Elegance, 2003, *Sculpted by Michael Evert, Open Edition*

g

Four Seasons

a. Spring Bouquet, 2003, *Sculpted by Sonja Bryer, Edition 2,000*
b. Winter Splendor, 2002, *Sculpted by Sonja Bryer, Edition 2,000*
c. Summer Breeze, 2002, *Sculpted by Sonja Bryer, Edition 2,000*
d. Autumn Harvest, 2002, *Sculpted by Sonja Bryer, Edition 2,000*

Nursery Rhyme Time

Dear to my Heart

Four Seasons Ballerina

a. This Little Piggy, 2002, *Sculpted by Kathy Smith-Fitzpatrick, Edition 5,000*

b. Shelby, 2002, *Sculpted by Adrienne Brown, Edition 1,500*

c. Natalya, 2001, *Sculpted by Linda Henry, Edition 1,500*

d. Francesca, 2002, *Sculpted by Linda Henry, Edition 1,500*

Four Seasons
Flowers

This series blossomed into something spectacular! In it, we celebrate the floral beauty of each of the four seasons.

a

b

a. Lilac, 2006, *Sculpted by Jo Ann Pohlman, Edition 2,000*
b. Poinsettia, 2005, *Sculpted by Sonja Bryer, Edition 2,000*

Always a
Bridesmaid

a. Patience, 2002, *Sculpted by Carole Bowling, Edition 2,500*

b. Faith, 2002, *Sculpted by Carole Bowling, Edition 2,500*

c. Hope, 2002, *Sculpted by Carole Bowling, Edition 2,500*

Artful Reflections

a

It's my opinion that dolls are works of art!

b

c

a. Alice, 2003, *Sculpted by Kathy Smith-Fitzpatrick, Edition 5,000*

b. Robin, 2003, *Sculpted by Lisa Jane, Edition 3,500*

c. Mademoiselle, 2004, *Sculpted by Kathy Smith-Fitzpatrick, Edition 750*

Captivating
in Color

Whether it's "Breathtaking in Blue," "Lovely in Lilac" or "Pretty in Periwinkle," these dolls, themed and named in colorful alliterations, are truly "Captivating in Color!"

a

c

b

a. Breathtaking in Blue, *2004, Sculpted by Ralph Bienert, Edition 6,000*

b. Lovely in Lilac, *2003, Sculpted by Kathy Smith-Fitzpatrick, Edition 1,500*

c. Pretty in Periwinkle, *2005, Sculpted by Jo Ann Pohlman, Edition 1,000*

Portrait

I love this series because each doll has a story and holds special meaning. Each story is heartfelt, and it's been my privilege to share these stories with my doll friends.

a

b

c

d

a. Judy Mae, 2003, *Sculpted by Sonja Bryer, Edition 2,000*
b. Mabel, 2004, *Sculpted by Karen Scott, Edition 300*
c. Daddy's Little Girl, 2005, *Sculpted by Sonja Bryer, Edition 1,500*
d. P.J., 2004, *Sculpted by Ping Lau, Edition 500*
e. Emmerson Rose, 2004, *Sculpted by Sonja Bryer, Edition 2,000*

e

Dear to My Heart

Toddlers

In 1991, I introduced you to a few of my dearest friends through my "Dear To My Heart" series. Now, 15 years later... my friends are getting younger! I'm happy to debut my new "Dear To My Heart Toddlers" collection with one of my best friends, "Baby Lisa." (Lisa and I celebrated 20 years of working together in May, 2005.)

a

a. Baby Lisa, 2006, Sculpted by Karen Scott, Edition 3,000

a. Marie at 3, 2005,
   Sculpted by Emily Garthright, Edition 10
b. Patricia Lynne, 2002,
   Sculpted by Marie Osmond, Edition 10
c. Heidi, 2001,
   Sculpted by Michele Severino, Edition 2,500
d. Sophia Brenn, 2004,
   Sculpted by Sonja Bryer, Edition 2,000

Miracle
Babies

Miracle
Children

a

a. Isobella, 2002, *Sculpted by Jessica Antoinette, Edition 1,000*

I sometimes think I was born in the wrong time period! While there is so much to love in our modern era, I do find myself drawn to by-gone generations . . . especially the clothing.

Changing Seasons

b. Emma Josefa & Rudy, 2002, *Sculpted by Sonja Bryer, Edition 2,500*

c. Cherise, 2001, *Sculpted by Jessica Antoinette, Edition, 5,000*

d. Collette - Winter / Summer, 2002, *Sculpted by Mary Benner, Edition 1,000*

e. Collette - Spring / Fall, 2005, *Sculpted by Mary Benner, Edition 1,000*

Classics

As a young girl, I fell in love with dolls from a by-gone era. The Bru dolls became my favorite as their faces are timeless, heirloom and indeed, classic.

a

b

c

d

a. Margaret, 2001, *Reproduction Bru Sculpt, Edition 500*

b. Justine, 2002, *Reproduction Bru Sculpt, Edition 1,000*

c. Jasmine, 2002, *Reproduction Bru Sculpt, Edition 1,000*

d. Aubrey, 2001, *Sculpted by Mary Benner, Edition 500*

e. Chika in Red, 2005, *Reproduction Bru Sculpt, Edition 100*

f. Chika, 2002, *Reproduction Bru Sculpt, Edition 2,000*

g. Chika in Blue, 2005, *Reproduction Bru Sculpt, Edition 150*

a

b

c

Victorian *Holiday*

There's no place like home for the holidays, especially when decorated with stunning and timeless treasures. I created these pieces to enrich and beautify your homes with the heirloom appeal of the Victorian era.

e

d

a. Chantal, *2006, Reproduction Cody Jumeau Sculpt, Edition 1,000*

b. Margarite, *2006, Reproduction Steiner Sculpt, Edition 1,000*

c. Katharina, *2006, Reproduction Mein Liebling Sculpt, Edition 1,000*

d. Monique, *2006, Reproduction Bru Sculpt, Edition 1,000*

e. Victorian Valentine, *2006, Sculpted by Karen Scott, Edition 500*

Classical Beauties

a. Kimberly-2006, 2006, *Sculpted by Beverly Stoehr, Edition 350*
b. Emma, 2001, *Sculpted by Jessica Antoinette, Edition 2,500*

Heartfelt

As an avid doll collector, I enjoy collecting many mediums of dolls and learning about each one. Felt dolls have a natural softness and warmth about them that make them truly, heartfelt.

a. Clarissa, 2001, *Sculpted by Carla Thompson, Edition 2,500*

b. Alleah, 2005, *Sculpted by Tawny Nix, Edition 250*

c. Olive May Heartfelt, 2004, *Sculpted by Marie Osmond, Edition 250*

d. *Kiana, 2003, Sculpted by Shirley Hunter Peck, Edition 750*
e. *Tawny, 2003, Sculpted by Tawny Nix, Edition 500*
f. *Baby Jessica Heartfelt, 2005, Sculpted by Beverly Stoehr, Edition 250*
g. *Baby Marie Heartfelt, 2005, Sculpted by Beverly Stoehr, Edition 500*

f

g

a

Toddler

In this, the evergreen series of my entire collection, I like to capture the sheer joy and happiness that our own babies bring into our lives. I create my "Toddler" dolls to evoke memories; to commemorate special occasions; to reflect hobbies and passions; to celebrate childhood. Each doll is designed with the hope that it will warm someone's heart and put a smile on their face. Relive your own memories, or create new ones with my "Toddlers"!

b

c

d

a. Baby Abigail, 2004,
   Sculpted by Sonja Bryer/Marie Osmond, Edition 5,000
b. Baby Abigail Blessing Day, 2005,
   Sculpted by Sonja Bryer/Marie Osmond, Edition 300
c. Baby Abigail in Pink, 2005,
   Sculpted by Sonja Bryer/Marie Osmond, Edition 500
d. Baby Abigail Crystal Anniversary, 2006,
   Sculpted by Sonja Bryer/Marie Osmond, Edition 300

a

b

(right) Baby Lisa Hatch and her beloved mother, Sue Hawkes.

c

d

a. Susie Loving Tribute, 2006, *Sculpted by Lisa Hatch, Edition 400*

b. Susie, 2004, *Sculpted by Lisa Hatch, Edition 1,000*

c. Susie Butterfly, 2005, *Sculpted by Lisa Hatch, Edition 500*

d. Susie Rose Bouquet, 2004, *Sculpted by Lisa Hatch, Edition 1,500*

e

f

g

e. M'Lissa Virginia, 2001, *Sculpted by Lisa Hatch, Edition 3,000*
f. M'Lissa Virginia Baby Blues, 2003, *Sculpted by Lisa Hatch, Edition 500*
g. M'Lissa Virginia Timeless, 2003, *Sculpted by Lisa Hatch, Edition 750*

a

b

c

a. Winter Blessing, 2004, *Sculpted by Karen Scott, Edition 1,500*

b. Bedtime Stories, 2004, *Sculpted by Penelope Carr, Edition 2,500*

c. All Toiled Up, 2003, *Sculpted by Sonja Bryer, Edition 3,500*

d. Belly Buttons and Bows, 2004, *Sculpted by Kathy Smith-Fitzpatrick, Edition 2,500*

e. Nia, 2001, *Sculpted by Adrienne Brown, Edition 5,000*

f. Baby Alexis Angel Kisses, 2003, *Sculpted by Lisa Hatch, Edition 2,000*

g. Sydney, 2003, *Sculpted by Karen Scott, Edition 1,000*

This is what doll collecting is all about...sharing it with the ones you love. Here I am with my daughter, Brianna, and her very own doll "Baby Brianna."

a. Baby Brianna Springtime, 2005, *Sculpted by Sonja Bryer, Edition 2,000*

b. Baby Brianna Holiday, 2005, *Sculpted by Sonja Bryer, Edition 400*

c. Baby Brianna, 2003, *Sculpted by Sonja Bryer, Edition 2,000*

d. Dusty Ann, *2005, Sculpted by Jo Ann Pohlman, Edition 3,000*
e. Ruffle Bum Baby, *2004, Sculpted by Jo Ann Pohlman, Edition 1,500*
f. Peggy, *2003, Sculpted by Karen Scott, Edition 1,500*

d

e

f

a. My Sister, 2005, *Sculpted by Jo Ann Pohlman, Edition 1,000*
b. Daisy Jane, 2004, *Sculpted by Jo Ann Pohlman, Edition 1,500*
c. Bottom's Up, 2005, *Sculpted by Jo Ann Pohlman, Edition 2,000*
d. Missy, 2001, *Sculpted by Michele Severino, Edition 5,000*

e. Diane, 2002, *Sculpted by Diane Vollmer, Edition 2,000*

f. Emmaline, 2005, *Sculpted by Karen Scott, Edition 2,000*

g. No, No, Nannette, 2003, *Sculpted by Jo Ann Pohlman, Edition 2,500*

h. Baby Miracles 2003, 2003, *Sculpted by Jo Ann Pohlman, Edition 2,003*

Not shown Helena, 2001, Neiman Marcus, Sculpted by Joke Grobben, Edition 500

a. Mommy's Girl, *2005, Sculpted by Karen Scott, Edition 750*

b. Sweet Freedom, *2005, Sculpted by Jo Ann Pohlman, Edition 750*

c. Ashley 2001, *2001, Sculpted by Beverly Stoehr, Edition 2,001*

d. Sunny Jo, *2003, Sculpted by Karen Scott, Edition 1,500*

e. Farmer's Daughter, *2004, Sculpted by Karen Scott, Edition 1,000*

f. Fay, *2002, Sculpted by Beverly Stoehr, Edition 2,500*

c

d

b

e

f

82

a. Boo Who?, 2005, *Sculpted by Karen Scott, Edition 2,000*

b. Candi Corn, 2004, *Sculpted by Jo Ann Pohlman, Edition 1,000*

c. Candi Cane, 2003, *Sculpted by Jo Ann Pohlman, Edition 500*

d. Amaya Holiday, 2002, *Sculpted by Sonja Bryer, Edition 5,000*

e. Let It Snow, 2004, *Sculpted by Sonja Bryer, Edition 2,000*

a

b

c

d

e

84

a. Holly Lolli, 2003, *Sculpted by Jo Ann Pohlman, Edition 2,500*
b. Lolli, 2002, *Sculpted by Jo Ann Pohlman, Edition 2,500*
c. Sugar Cookie, 2005, *Sculpted by Jo Ann Pohlman, Edition 1,000*

a

b

c

d. Christmas Cookie, 2004, *Sculpted by Jo Ann Pohlman, Edition 1,000*

e. Cotton Candi, 2004, *Sculpted by Jo Ann Pohlman, Edition 1,500*

f. I Love You Lolli, 2002, *Sculpted by Jo Ann Pohlman, Edition 2,500*

g. Smart Cookie, 2005, *Sculpted by Jo Ann Pohlman, Edition 1,000*

a. Shao Mei, 2004, *Sculpted by Ping Lau, Edition 2,500*

b. Li Ying, 2004, *Sculpted by Ping Lau, Edition 3,000*

c. Shao Pang, 2002, *Sculpted by Ping Lau, Edition 3,000*

d. Summer Sunshine, 2003, *Sculpted by Michele Severino, Edition 2,500*

e. Spring Daisy, 2003, *Sculpted by Michele Severino, Edition 2,500*

b

c

d

e

got milk?®

a. got milk?, 2003, *Sculpted by Jo Ann Pohlman, Edition 5,000*

b. got chocolate milk?, 2005, *Sculpted by Jo Ann Pohlman, Edition 3,000*

"got milk?" is a registered trademark of the California Milk Processor Board.

Strawberry Shortcake™

I fell in love with Strawberry Shortcake in the 1980's, and now, all these years later, I love sharing Strawberryland with my own daughters. Strawberry Shortcake is a sweet, spunky and adventurous red-head who celebrates the joys of each day and encourages little girls to be little girls . . . and big girls to be little girls again!

a. Strawberry Shortcake, 2005, *Sculpted by Ping Lau, Edition 5,000*
b. Blueberry Muffin, 2005, *Sculpted by Ping Lau, Edition 2,500*
c. Raspberry Tart, 2006, *Sculpted by Ping Lau, Edition 2,500*

With our adorable Hershey's dolls, I combine two of my all-time favorite things . . . dolls and chocolate. Does it get any better than this?!

HERSHEY'S

a. Merry Kisses, 2005, *Sculpted by Ping Lau, Edition 2,500*
b. KISSES® Tiny Tot, 2006, *Sculpted by Ping Lau, Open Edition*
c. HERSHEY'S HUGS™, 2005, *Sculpted by Ping Lau, Edition 2,500*
d. Caramel KISSES®, 2005, *Sculpted by Ping Lau, Edition 2,500*
e. KISSES®, 2004, *Sculpted by Ping Lau, Edition 5,000*

e

KISSES, the conical configuration and plume device are trademarks used under license by Charisma Brands licensee.

92

Disney *Babies*

Disney and my family go way back, starting with my brothers being discovered by Andy William's father at Disneyland where they were singing barbershop melodies. It's a tradition I'm proud to carry on with my magical "Disney Babies."

a. The One and Only Cinderella, *2005, Sculpted by Sonja Bryer, Edition 1*

b

c

b. Sleeping Beauty 50th Anniversary, *2005,*
   Sculpted by Sonja Bryer, Edition 300

c. Baby Snow White 65th Anniversary, *2002,*
   Sculpted by Sonja Bryer, Edition 3,600

d. Pixie Dusted Tink, *2004,*
   Sculpted by Sonja Bryer, Edition 500

e. Baby Annette 50th Anniversary, *2005,*
   Sculpted by Sonja Bryer, Edition 300

f. Cinderella 50th Anniversary, *2005,*
   Sculpted by Sonja Bryer, Edition 300

d

e

f

c

a. Baby Queen of Hearts, 2004,
   Sculpted by Sonja Bryer, Open Edition
b. Baby Tinker Bell 50th Anniversary, 2002,
   Sculpted by Sonja Bryer, Open Edition
c. Baby Mary Poppins, 2004,
   Sculpted by Sonja Bryer, Open Edition
d. Baby Cruella, 2002,
   Sculpted by Sonja Bryer, Open Edition

d

e

f

e. Baby Belle 10th Anniversary, 2002,
   Sculpted by Sonja Bryer, Edition 1,000
f. Snow White Snow Flake, 2001,
   Sculpted by Sonja Bryer, Edition 1
g. Baby Christmas Belle Trio, 2001,
   Sculpted by Sonja Bryer, Edition 50
   (Collectible plaque not shown)

g

a. Baby Annette Holiday, 2004, *Sculpted by Jo Ann Pohlman, Edition 3,000*

b. Baby Annette, 2003, *Sculpted by Jo Ann Pohlman, Edition 5,000*

c. Clara, 2002, *Sculpted by Karen Scott, Edition 5,000*

d. Bear Hugs & Kissy, 2004, *Sculpted by Marie Osmond, Edition 2,500*

Quite A Pair

This series, for me, has been creatively rewarding as I've been privileged to collaborate with several of my collectible industry friends. We make "Quite a Pair," don't you think?! (smiles)

e

f

g

e. Adora Belle Baby, 2004,
   Sculpted by Marie Osmond, Edition 5,000

f. Basket & Blooms Baby, 2003,
   Sculpted by Sonja Bryer, Edition 3,500

g. Beary Bitty Ballerina, 2004,
   Sculpted by Marie Osmond/Annette Funicello, Open Edition

a. Blossom, 2004, Sculpted by Ping Lau, Open Edition

Babies a Bloom

After eight children of my own and nearly 80 nieces and nephews, it's safe to say that I have become an expert baby cuddler, so I set out to design a line of dolls that realistically replicates the cuddleability of a real child. After three years of intensive product development, we finally achieved it! "Babies-a-Bloom", with it's "Cuddle Me" vinyl, moves dolls into the next generation of playability and collectibility.

b. Daisy, 2004, *Sculpted by Ping Lau, Open Edition*

c. Butterpillar, 2005, *Sculpted by Ping Lau, Open Edition*

d. Sweet Pea, 2005, *Sculpted by Ping Lau, Open Edition*

e. Lil' Slugger, 2005, *Sculpted by Ping Lau, Open Edition*

f. Pansy, 2005, *Sculpted by Ping Lau, Open Edition*

a. Birthday Bloom - African American, 2005, *Sculpted by Ping Lau, Open Edition*

b. Birthday Bloom - Blonde, 2005, *Sculpted by Ping Lau, Open Edition*

c. Birthday Bloom - Brunette, 2005, *Sculpted by Ping Lau, Open Edition*

Babies a bloom

d. Lil' Pumpkin, 2005, *Sculpted by Ping Lau, Open Edition*
e. Snowflake, 2005, *Sculpted by Ping Lau, Open Edition*
f. Poppy, 2005, *Sculpted by Ping Lau, Open Edition*

Children's Miracle Network is a non-profit organization dedicated to saving and improving the lives of children by raising funds for children's hospitals. Since founding CMN in 1983, we have raised over 2.5 billion dollars, thanks in large part to the generosity of friends like you. Thank You!

a

Collectible dolls
You'll love to play with...

Babies
a
bloom

Play dolls
You'll love to collect!

a. Miracles-A-Bloom, 2005, *Sculpted by Ping Lau, Open Edition*
b. Holly, 2004, *Sculpted by Ping Lau, Open Edition*

b

Expressions
of Love

We all say them . . . those endearing little expressions of love reserved for addressing those we hold most dear.

a

b

a. Nuts About You, 2004, *Sculpted by Diane Vollmer, Edition 1,000*
b. Love Bug, 2005, *Sculpted by Jo Ann Pohlman, Edition 1,500*
c. I Love Ewe, 2002, *Sculpted by Penelope Carr, Edition 5,000*
d. I Piqué You, 2004, *Sculpted by Caroli Gardiner, Edition 500*

c

d

a

b

c

Dolls are very personal for me, and for most doll collectors I know. Many times they represent memories of some of my favorite things...like bedtime kisses to my babies; or getting them ready for church on Sunday morning; or playing dolls. These are a few of my favorite things!

a. Bedtime Kisses, 2005, *Sculpted by Jo Ann Pohlman, Edition 750*
b. May Flowers, 2003, *Sculpted by Jo Ann Pohlman, Edition 2,000*
c. Butterfly Kisses, 2002, *Sculpted by Jo Ann Pohlman, Edition 2,500*
d. Playing Dolls, 2005, *Sculpted by Jo Ann Pohlman, Edition 750*
e. Chasing Rainbows, 2003, *Sculpted by Jo Ann Pohlman, Edition 850*
f. What's Cookin?, 2004, *Sculpted by Jo Ann Pohlman, Edition 750*

a. April Showers, *2003, Sculpted by Jo Ann Pohlman, Edition 2,000*
b. Sweet Dreams, *2003, Sculpted by Jo Ann Pohlman, Edition 2,000*
c. Blowing Kisses, *2004, Sculpted by Jo Ann Pohlman, Edition 750*
d. Sunday Morning, *2005, Sculpted by Jo Ann Pohlman, Edition 1,000*

Dolls
for all
Seasons

a. A Doll For All Seasons/2, 2001, *Sculpted by Michele Severino, Edition 2,500*

b. A Doll For All Seasons/3, 2001, *Sculpted by Michele Severino, Open Edition*
   (*Valentine Doll Not Shown*)

c. A Doll For All Seasons, 2000, *Sculpted by Michele Severino, Edition 2,500*

Beary Special *Babies*

Musical Moments

a. Beary Special Baby Boy, 2002,
   Sculpted by Jo Ann Pohlman, Edition 2,000

b. Beary Special Baby Girl, 2002,
   Sculpted by Jo Ann Pohlman, Edition 2,000

c. We Wish You A Merry Christmas, 2004,
   Sculpted by Sonja Bryer, Edition 1,500

d. Put On A Happy Face, 2004,
   Sculpted by Sonja Bryer, Edition 2,000

First Things First

Babies are one of life's greatest blessings, and there is no joy that can equal that of witnessing them first crawl, or play peek-a-boo, or take their first step.

a. Baby Steps, 2005, *Sculpted by Jo Ann Pohlman, Edition 2,000*

b. Patty Cake, 2005, *Sculpted by Jo Ann Pohlman, Edition 2,000*

c. Here Comes Trouble, 2004, *Sculpted by Jo Ann Pohlman, Edition 2,000*

LENOX

Since 1889, Lenox has created beautiful gifts, tableware and collectibles, including being the first American china to be used in the White House. I am pleased to collaborate with Lenox to bring you elegant dolls whose dresses were created to embody the timeless and classic appeal of Lenox.

a

b

c

d

e

f

a. Baby's 1st Christmas 2003, *2003,*
   Sculpted by Sonja Bryer, Edition 500
b. Happy Birthday, *2004,*
   Sculpted by Sonja Bryer, Edition 500
c. Holiday Elegance, *2005,*
   Sculpted by Karen Scott, Edition 500

d. Baby's 1st Birthday 2003, *2003,*
   Sculpted by Sonja Bryer, Edition 500
e. Happy Holidays, *2004,*
   Sculpted by Sonja Bryer, Edition 500
f. Timeless, *2005,*
   Sculpted by Karen Scott, Edition 750

Not Shown Baby's First Christmas, 2002

Artist Portrait

a. Baby Beverly Virginia, *2006, Sculpted by Beverly Stoehr, Edition 1,500*

I am so excited to bring you this series! To commemorate our 15th Anniversary, I commissioned my good friends and fellow doll sculptors to sculpt themselves as babies . . . just for you. Collecting doesn't get any better than this!

Fun Fruits

I agree with the recommendation that a person should have 5 servings of fruit each day (plus an extra helping for good measure)! Fruit is sweet, but "Fun Fruits" are even sweeter!

a

b

a. Lizzy Lemon, 2002,
   Sculpted by Jo Ann Pohlman, Edition 2,500
b. Sherry Cherry, 2002,
   Sculpted by Jo Ann Pohlman, Edition 2,500
c. Franny Fruit Basket, 2003,
   Sculpted by Jo Ann Pohlman, Edition 2,500

c

d. Stacey Strawberry, 2002,
   Sculpted by Jo Ann Pohlman, Edition 2,500
e. Apple Annie, 2002,
   Sculpted by Jo Ann Pohlman, Edition 2,500
f. Boyz N' Berry, 2003,
   Sculpted by Jo Ann Pohlman, Edition 2,500

114

Fruit Cls

One of the highlights of Summer and Autumn is savoring the sweetness of fresh-picked fruit. I can almost taste strawberry shortcake or mixed fruit salad, or warm cherry cobbler . . . with vanilla ice cream on top, of course!

c

b

d

e

f

Sweet Treats

g

a. Franny Fruit Basket Fruit Cup, 2005, *Sculpted by Jo Ann Pohlman, Open Edition*
b. Apple Annie Fruit Cup, 2004, *Sculpted by Jo Ann Pohlman, Open Edition*
c. Lizzy Lemon Fruit Cup, 2004, *Sculpted by Jo Ann Pohlman, Open Edition*
d. Boyz N Berry Fruit Cup, 2004, *Sculpted by Jo Ann Pohlman, Open Edition*
e. Stacey Strawberry Fruit Cup, 2004, *Sculpted by Jo Ann Pohlman, Open Edition*
f. Sherry Cherry Fruit Cup, 2004, *Sculpted by Jo Ann Pohlman, Open Edition*
g. Cherries Jubilee, 2004, *Sculpted by Jo Ann Pohlman, Edition 2,000*

You're
Bugging Me

b

a

Costumed and themed in bug-print fabrics, "You're Bugging Me" is a playful, double-entendre collection that gives new meaning to the expression— you're bugging me!

a. Ladylike, 2005, *Sculpted by Sonja Bryer, Edition 750*

b. Ants In My Pants, 2004, *Sculpted by Sonja Bryer, Edition 2,000*

c. You're Bugging Me, 2005, *Sculpted by Sonja Bryer, Edition 2,000*

d. Bee in My Bonnet, 2004, *Sculpted by Sonja Bryer, Edition 2,000*

e. Butterflies In My Tummy, 2004, *Sculpted by Sonja Bryer, Edition 2,000*

Bitty *Beauty Bugs*

Some of you remember the song, "Ugly Bug Ball." Well, one day I had the notion that bugs were getting a bad rap, so I decided to turn the tables and give them a chance to show their beautiful sides. Not only are my bugs beautiful...they're also regal!

a. Queen Bee Bitty Beauty Bug, *2005, Sculpted by Linda Henry, Open Edition*

b. Madame Butterfly Bitty Beauty Bug, *2005, Sculpted by Linda Henry, Open Edition*

c. Countess Caterpillar Bitty Beauty Bug, *2005, Sculpted by Linda Henry, Open Edition*

d. Count Cocky Cockroach Bitty Beauty Bug, *2005, Sculpted by Linda Henry, Open Edition*

e. Lady Bug Bitty Beauty Bug, *2005, Sculpted by Linda Henry, Open Edition*

f. Baroness Von Beetle Bitty Beauty Bug, *2006, Sculpted by Linda Henry, Open Edition*

g. Baron Von Beetle Bitty Beauty Bug, *2006, Sculpted by Linda Henry, Open Edition*

h. Miss Quito Bitty Beauty Bug, *2006, Sculpted by Linda Henry, Open Edition*

i. Sir Stinkbug Bitty Beauty Bug, *2006, Sculpted by Linda Henry, Open Edition*

j. Damsel Dragonfly Bitty Beauty Bug, *2006, Sculpted by Linda Henry, Open Edition*

a

b

Bitty
Bunnies

d

a. Hareloom Bitty Bunny, *2004,*
   Sculpted by Linda Henry, Open Edition

b. Rosemarie & Robbie Rabbit Bitty Bunnies, *2005,*
   Sculpted by Linda Henry, Open Edition

c. Santa Bunny & Mrs. Paws Bitty Bunnies, *2003,*
   Sculpted by Linda Henry, Open Edition

d. Fuzzy Baby & Hareiat Bitty Bunnies, *2004,*
   Sculpted by Linda Henry, Open Edition

c

Tiny Tots

Next to my "Toddler" collection, these tiny dolls are my biggest series! The ever popular "Tiny Tots" are perfect in every way and make collecting and displaying dolls . . . no _Big_ deal!

a. All Toiled Up Tiny Tot, 2006, Sculpted by Sonja Bryer, Open Edition

b. Savannah Marie Tiny Tot, 2003,
   Sculpted by Marie Osmond, Open Edition
c. Olive May Twosome, 2002,
   Sculpted by Marie Osmond, Open Edition
d. Baby Marie Paper Roses Tiny Tot, 2002,
   Sculpted by Beverly Stoehr, Open Edition

e. Baby Beverly Tiny Tot, 2003,
   Sculpted by Beverly Stoehr, Open Edition
f. Baby Miss America Tiny Tot, 2004,
   Sculpted by Sonja Bryer, Edition 1,200
g. got milk? Tiny Tot, 2005,
   Sculpted by Jo Ann Pohlman, Open Edition
h. Baby Marie Picture Day Tiny Tot, 2004,
   Sculpted by Beverly Stoehr, Open Edition

a. Generations Tiny Tot Trio, 2001,
   Sculpted by Osmond/Stoehr, Open Edition
b. Beary Best Friends Tiny Tot, 2002,
   Sculpted by Sonja Bryer, Open Edition
c. Amaya Springtime Tiny Tot, 2003,
   Sculpted by Sonja Bryer, Open Edition

d. Suzanne Tiny Tot, 2003,
   Sculpted by Maryse Nicole, Open Edition
e. I'll Love You Till The Cows Come Home Tiny Tot, 2002,
   Sculpted by Rita Schmidt, Open Edition
f. Saundra Tiny Tot, 2003,
   Sculpted by Carole Bowling, Open Edition

g. Claudia Tiny Tot, 2005,
   Reproduction K & R Sculpt, Open Edition
h. Baby Wizard of Oz Tiny Tot, 2002,
   Sculpted by Sonja Bryer, Open Edition
i. Daisy Tiny Tot, 2001,
   Sculpted by Marie Osmond, Open Edition
j. Jessica Tiny Tot, 2001, *Sculpted by Vincent De Filippo, Open Edition*

k. Sheila Tiny Tot, 2003,
   Sculpted by Berdine Creedy, Open Edition
l. Sunshine & Happiness Tiny Tot, 2002,
   Sculpted by Beverly Stoehr, Open Edition
m. Grandma Kit Tiny Tot, 2005,
   Sculpted by Cheryl Robinson Reproduction Wolfie Sculpt, Edition 500
n. Rachael Tiny Tot, 2002,
   Anonymous Sculptor, Open Edition

124

a. Very Beary In Love Tiny Tot, 2005, *Anonymous Sculptor, Open Edition*
b. From Caterpillars To Butterflies Tiny Tot, 2002, *Sculpted by Sonja Bryer, Open Edition*
c. Puppy Love Tiny Tot, 2005, *Sculpted by Beverly Stoehr, Open Edition*
d. Angelica's First Birthday Tiny Tot, 2002, *Sculpted by Beverly Stoehr, Open Edition*

e. Rylee Tiny Tot, 2003,
   Sculpted by Sandra Babin, Open Edition
f. Hansel & Gretel Tiny Tots, 2002,
   Sculpted by Beverly Stoehr, Open Edition
g. Ena Tiny Tot, 2004,
   Sculpted by Carole Bowling, Open Edition

h. Lolli Tiny Tot, 2004,
Sculpted by Jo Ann Pohlman, Open Edition

i. Peek-A-Boo Tiny Tot, 2003,
Sculpted by Marie Osmond, Open Edition

j. Cotton Candi Tiny Tot, 2005,
Sculpted by Jo Ann Pohlman, Open Edition

k. Mary Sunshine Tiny Tot, 2003,
Sculpted by Beverly Stoehr, Open Edition

l. I Love You Lolli Tiny Tot, 2006,
Sculpted by Jo Ann Pohlman, Open Edition

m. Bryanna Tiny Tot, 2003,
Sculpted by Rita Schmidt, Open Edition

a. Santa Baby Tiny Tot, 2001,
   Sculpted by Sonja Bryer, Open Edition
b. Ann Marie Holiday Tiny Tot, 2002,
   Sculpted by Sonja Bryer, Open Edition
c. Helena Tiny Tot, 2005,
   Sculpted by Joke Grobben, Open Edition

d. M'Lissa Virginia Tiny Tot Trio, 2004,
   Sculpted by Lisa Hatch, Open Edition
e. Clara Tiny Tot, 2004,
   Sculpted by Karen Scott, Open Edition
f. Angel Baby Tiny Tot Trio, 2002,
   Sculpted by Sonja Bryer, Open Edition
g. Winter Blessing Tiny Tot, 2005,
   Sculpted by Karen Scott, Open Edition

h. Baby Alice In Wonderland Tiny Tot, *2001*,
   Sculpted by Sonja Bryer, Open Edition

i. Baby Tinker Bell Tiny Tot, *2004*,
   Sculpted by Sonja Bryer, Open Edition

j. Rosie & Rags as Mickey & Minnie Christmas Tiny Tots, *2001*,
   Sculpted by Beverly Stoehr, Open Edition

k. Rosie & Rags Tiny Tots, *2002*,
   Sculpted by Beverly Stoehr, Open Edition

l. Rosie & Rags as Mickey & Minnie Tiny Tots, *2001*,
   Sculpted by Beverly Stoehr, Open Edition

m. Baby Mulan Tiny Tot, *2002*,
   Sculpted by Sonja Bryer, Open Edition

n. Snow White Snow Flake Tiny Tot, *2001*,
   Sculpted by Sonja Bryer, Open Edition

Tiny Triplets

a. Tiny Teddy, 2005, *Sculpted by Karen Scott, Edition 2,000*

b. Tiny TuTu, 2005, *Sculpted by Karen Scott, Edition 2,000*

c. Tiny Tears, 2005, *Sculpted by Karen Scott, Edition 2,000*

Tinier Tots

d. Small Dolls For All Seasons - Pumpkin, Turkey, Christmas, 2002, *Sculpted by Michele Severino, Open Edition*

e. Small Dolls For All Seasons - 4th of July, Easter, Valentine, 2003, *Sculpted by Michele Severino, Open Edition*

Tiny Dancers

Tu – Tu cute! Every time I see these dolls,
I laugh! I hope the memories of my own
children's early dance recitals never fade away!

a. Oh! You Beautiful Doll, 2004,
  Sculpted by Jo Ann Pohlman, Edition 2,000

b. Edelwiess, 2003,
  Sculpted by Jo Ann Pohlman, Edition 2,500

c. Ballerina Girl, 2003,
  Sculpted by Jo Ann Pohlman, Edition 5,000

d. Here Comes Santa Claus, 2003,
  Sculpted by Jo Ann Pohlman, Edition 2,000

e. Good Ship Lollipop, 2003,
  Sculpted by Jo Ann Pohlman, Edition 2,500

f. Send In The Clowns, 2003,
  Sculpted by Jo Ann Pohlman, Edition 2,500

California Girls

Music has played such a huge role in my life. With the "California Girls" series, I wanted to have a little fun interpreting one of my favorite Beach Boys tunes.

a. Northern Girl, 2001,
   Dotty Darling Reproduction Sculpt, Edition 5,000

b. Mid-West Girl, 2001,
   Dotty Darling Reproduction Sculpt, Edition 5,000

c. Hawaiian Island Girl, 2002,
   Dotty Darling Reproduction Sculpt, Edition 5,000

d. East Coast Girl, 2001,
   Dotty Darling Reproduction Sculpt, Edition 5,000

e. Southern Girl, 2002,
   Dotty Darling Reproduction Sculpt, Edition 5,000

f. California Girl, 2001,
   Dotty Darling Reproduction Sculpt, Edition 5,000

Three's A Charm

a

Good things come in series of 3's, starting with the "Three Little Kittens." Like so many of you, I'm a cat lover, so I commissioned Ping Lau to sculpt a set of childlike faces for my kitty trio, and I think you'll agree that the end result is, well . . . charming!

a. Fluffy, 2006, Sculpted by Ping Lau, Edition 2,000

Ice Cream Kids

While compiling this book, I realized just how many of my dolls are related to food! What does that say about me? I hope it says that I love life enough o enjoy food . . . especially ice cream!

a. Mint Chip 2005, *Sculpted by Jo Ann Pohlman, Edition 1,500*

b. Rainbow Sherbet, 2005, *Sculpted by Jo Ann Pohlman, Edition 1,500*

c. Cherry Vanilla, 2004, *Sculpted by Jo Ann Pohlman, Edition 1,500*

d. Rocky Road, 2005, *Sculpted by Jo Ann Pohlman, Edition 1,500*

Boys Will Be Boys
Girls Will Be Girls

b

a

With this series, we wanted to capture the unmistakable nature of little boys, (note the snowball ready to be thrown?) and little girls . . . or at least how we envision them to be!

c

d

a. Boys Will Be Boys/Girls Will Be Girls - Spring, *2005, Anonymous Sculptor, Edition 1,500*
b. Boys Will Be Boys/Girls Will Be Girls - Summer, *2004, Anonymous Sculptor, Edition 1,500*
c. Boys Will Be Boys/Girls Will Be Girls - Fall, *2005, Anonymous Sculptor, Edition 1,500*
d. Boys Will Be Boys/Girls Will Be Girls - Winter, *2004, Anonymous Sculptor, Edition 1,500*

Petite Amour
Toddlers

a

b

c

d

e

All good things must come to an end. In 2003, we retired one of my all-time favorite series, the very detailed, ever-adorable "Petite Amour Toddlers." (I'll miss you the most, "Pumpkin & Patches!" Smiles.)

a. King and Queen of Hearts, 2003, *Anonymous Sculptor, Edition 2,500*

b. Uncle Sam & Libby, 2002, *Anonymous Sculptor, Edition 2,500*

c. Pumpkin & Patches, 2002, *Anonymous Sculptor, Edition 2,500*

d. Hansel & Gretel, 2001, *Anonymous Sculptor, Edition 2,500*

e. Heroes, 2003, *Anonymous Sculptor, Edition 2,500*

f. Jack & Jill, 2001, *Anonymous Sculptor, Edition 2,500*

g. St. Paddy & His Bonnie Lass, 2003, *Anonymous Sculptor, Edition 2,500*

h. Peace On Earth, 2003, *Anonymous Sculptor, Edition 2,500*

i. Kris & Kriscinda Kringle, 2002, *Anonymous Sculptor, Edition 5,000*

Waxallure

As an avid collector, I'm attracted to various mediums of dolls . . . porcelain, vinyl, felt, resin, wood, and wax. There is a life-like quality that radiates from a wax doll that I find very appealing.

a. Nikela, 2002, *Sculpted by Carole Bowling, Edition 500*
b. Little Jack Horner, 2003, *Sculpted by Joann Gelin, Edition 2,000*
c. Little Miss Muffet, 2003, *Sculpted by Joann Gelin, Edition 2,000*
d. Adora Belle Allure, 2005, *Sculpted by Marie Osmond, Edition 300*

Greeting Card

Collectible Greeting

a. Enlightened, 2003, *Artwork by Nelda Pieper, Open Edition*

b. Doll Magic, 2003, *Artwork by Tom Browning, Open Edition*

c. Confidant, 2002, *Sculpted by Susan Scogin/Artwork by Greg Olsen, Open Edition*

d. 4 Letter Words To Live By, 2002, *Sculpted by Debbie Sampson, Edition 1,000*

Sentiments

La Femme Statuette

a

b

a. Ashlyn, *2003, Sculpted by Sonja Bryer, Edition 1,000*

b. Amelia, *2002, Sculpted by Elisa, Edition 2,000*

c. Angel Baby Boy, *2002, Sculpted by Sonja Bryer, Edition 1,200*

d. Noelle, *2001, Sculpted by Michele Severino, Edition 1,000*

New Millenium

Christmas Carolers

c

d

Baby Me

a

b

c

a. Baby Me - Auburn, 2006, *Sculpted by Karen Scott, Edition 300*
b. Baby Me - Brunette, 2006, *Sculpted by Karen Scott, Edition 300*
c. Baby Me - Blonde, 2006, *Sculpted by Karen Scott, Edition 300*
d. Scooter Pie, 2002, *Anonymous Sculptor, Open Edition*
e. Gone Fishin', 2001, *Anonymous Sculptor, Open Edition*

Little Me

d

e

Dolls Around the World

Having had the opportunity to travel the world since I was a child, I have first-hand appreciation for the unique beauty of many cultures . . . their customs and their costuming, which served as inspiration for my "Dolls Around the World" collection.

a. China Girl, 2004, *Sculpted by Ping Lau, Open Edition*

b. Russian Girl, 2004, *Sculpted by Ping Lau, Open Edition*

c. USA Girl, 2004, *Sculpted by Ping Lau, Open Edition*

d. Ireland Girl, 2004, *Sculpted by Ping Lau, Open Edition*

e. Brazil Girl, 2004, *Sculpted by Ping Lau, Open Edition*

f. South African Girl, 2004, *Sculpted by Ping Lau, Open Edition*

g. Taki, 2002, *Sculpted by Carole Bowling, Edition 2,500*

Children of the World

a

b

c

d

These dolls make me smile, and I hope they bring a smile to your face as well. A fun interpretation of rag-a-muffins, using rag dolls and muffin flavors, these are the low-carb, high-cuteness muffins!

a. Blueberry Muffin, *2005, Sculpted by Marie Osmond, Open Edition*
b. Lemon Poppyseed, *2005, Sculpted by Marie Osmond, Open Edition*
c. Pumpkin Spice, *2005, Sculpted by Marie Osmond, Open Edition*
d. Oatmeal Raisin, *2006, Sculpted by Marie Osmond, Open Edition*

Twins

I've never outgrown the love of rag dolls! There is just something about their yarn, mop-top hair and painted noses that keeps me in "stitches." Kissy & Huggs to all my fellow doll lovers!

a

b

c

a. Kissy & Huggs, *2003, Sculpted by Marie Osmond, Edition 15,000*
b. French Kissy, *2005, Sculpted by Marie Osmond, Edition 500*
c. Kissy & Huggs Mistle Ho Ho Ho, *2003, Sculpted by Marie Osmond, Edition 6,000*

d. Eskimo Kissy, 2005, *Sculpted by Marie Osmond, Edition 500*

e. Kissy & Huggs Red, White & I Love Blue, 2004,
   Sculpted by Marie Osmond, Edition 3,000

f. Kissy & Huggs Little Bit Country, 2004,
   Sculpted by Marie Osmond, Edition 1,500

144

Wee Bees

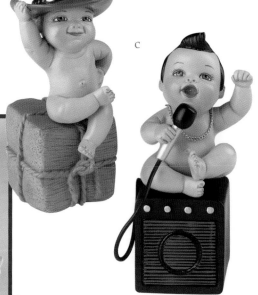

It's true that good things come in small packages, and as proof... I offer you my "Wee Bees." These petite resin dolls are an unexpected surprise when measured against other such collectibles. They are a breath of sunshine to your collection... your home... your life; reminding us to smile every now and then.

a. Ebony & Ivory, 2005, *Sculpted by Ping Lau, Open Edition*

b. Loves Me/Loves Me Not, 2004, *Sculpted by Ping Lau, Open Edition*

c. Little Bit Country/Rock & Roll, 2005, *Sculpted by Ping Lau, Open Edition*

d. Hugs & Kisses, 2004, *Sculpted by Ping Lau, Open Edition*

e. Naughty & Nice, 2003, *Sculpted by Ping Lau, Open Edition*

f. Hear, See, Speak No Evil, 2003, *Sculpted by Ping Lau, Open Edition*

g. Sunrise and Sunset, 2004, *Sculpted by Ping Lau, Open Edition*

ADORA *Belle*

a. Baby Adora Santa Belle, 2004,
   Sculpted by Marie Osmond, Edition 1,000

a

146

Baby Adora Belle

As a young girl, I had posters on my wall of a wide-eyed, character-like doll. Her unique proportions and features intrigued me, and served as my inspiration when I sculpted Adora Belle. We debuted Adora Belle in 1997, and since that time, she's appeared in many adorable themes, making her one of the hallmark series within my doll line. She's simply "Adora Belle!"

a

ADORA *Belle*

a. Baby Cuddle Me Adora Belle, 2005,
   Sculpted by Marie Osmond, Edition 3,000

b. Adora Belle Baby, 2004,
   Sculpted by Marie Osmond, Edition 5,000

c. Baby Adora My Doll Friend, 2005,
   Sculpted by Marie Osmond, Edition 300

d. Baby Adora Holly Belle, 2004,
   Sculpted by Marie Osmond, Edition 5,000

148

a

b

c

d

a. Udderly Adora Belle, *2005, Sculpted by Marie Osmond, Open Edition*
b. Dog Gone Adora Belle, *2006, Sculpted by Marie Osmond, Open Edition*
c. Adora My Dolly, *2004, Sculpted by Marie Osmond, Open Edition*
d. Adora Irish Belle, *2005, Sculpted by Marie Osmond, Open Edition*

e. Horror-A-Belle and Terri Beau, 2004, *Sculpted by Marie Osmond, Open Edition*

f. Adora Bitty Boo, 2003, *Sculpted by Marie Osmond, Open Edition*

g. Adora School Belle and Beau, 2003, *Sculpted by Marie Osmond, Open Edition*

h. Amour-A-Belle and Beau, 2005, *Sculpted by Marie Osmond, Open Edition*

i. Come Let Us Adora Him, 2005, *Sculpted by Marie Osmond, Open Edition*

j. Adora Belle & Beau Nautical & Nice, 2003, *Sculpted by Marie Osmond, Open Edition*

Adora Belle

a

ADORA *Belle*

a. Love-A-Belle, 2003,
   Sculpted by Marie Osmond, Open Edition

b. Adora Beau Groom, 2002,
   Sculpted by Marie Osmond, Open Edition

c. Adora Belle Sweetheart, 2002,
   Sculpted by Marie Osmond, Edition 1,000

d. Adora My Friends, 2005,
   Sculpted by Marie Osmond, Edition 150

a. Adora Belle Spring Fling - Aqua, 2003,
Sculpted by Marie Osmond, Open Edition

b. Adora Belle Spring Fling - Peach, 2003,
Sculpted by Marie Osmond, Open Edition

c. Adora Belle Easter, 2002,
Sculpted by Marie Osmond, Open Edition

d. Butterfly Belle, 2002,
Sculpted by Marie Osmond, Edition 1,000

"Adora Belle-Doll for the Cure" is a beautiful doll for a beautiful cause. I am pleased to partner with FFANY to help raise awareness and funds for breast cancer research and education, to which a portion of the proceeds are donated. Wearing a dress of pink satin with a dotted-Swiss overlay, and a pink ribbon-esque wrap secured by an official breast cancer awareness pin, she's not just adorable, she's "Adora Belle-Doll for the Cure."

e. Adora My Teddy, 2002,
   Sculpted by Marie Osmond, Open Edition

f. Adora Belle-Doll for the Cure, 2005,
   Sculpted by Marie Osmond, Edition 3,000

FF_aNY

FFANY

Founded in 1979, The Fashion Footwear Association of New York (FFANY) was organized as a non-profit trade association, committed to philanthropy. Since that date, FFANY has raised over $16 million for breast cancer research and education.

154

a

a. Adora Belle as Gwenivere, 2003, *Sculpted by Marie Osmond, Open Edition*
b. Adora Belle Angel 2004, 2004, *Sculpted by Marie Osmond, Edition 2,000*
c. Adora Belle of the Ball, 2002, *Sculpted by Marie Osmond, Open Edition*
d. Adora Belle Snow Princess, 2003, *Sculpted by Marie Osmond, Edition 500*
e. Adora Angelique, 2002, *Sculpted by Marie Osmond, Edition 750*

b

c

d

e

a

b

c

d

e

f

a. Adora Belle Holiday 2005, *2005, Sculpted by Marie Osmond, Open Edition*
b. Adora Belle Holiday 2002, *2002, Sculpted by Marie Osmond, Open Edition*
c. Adora Belle Holiday 2001, *2001, Sculpted by Marie Osmond, Open Edition*
d. Adora Belle Holiday 2003, *2003, Sculpted by Marie Osmond, Open Edition*
e. Adora Belle Heaven Sent, *2002, Sculpted by Marie Osmond, Open Edition*
f. Adora Belle Holiday 2004, *2004, Sculpted by Marie Osmond, Open Edition*

a

b

c

d

ADORA Belle

159

a. Adora Belles & Whistles - Pretty In Pink, 2004, *Sculpted by Marie Osmond, Edition 500*

b. Adora Belle of Freedom, 2002, *Sculpted by Marie Osmond, Open Edition*

c. Adora Belle - Let Freedom Ring, 2004, *Sculpted by Marie Osmond, Open Edition*

d. Adora Belles & Whistles, 2004, *Sculpted by Marie Osmond, Edition 500*

e. Adora Little Devil, 2005, *Sculpted by Marie Osmond, Edition 500*

f. Adora Boo, 2002, *Sculpted by Marie Osmond, Open Edition*

g. Adora Kitty Belle, 2004, *Sculpted by Marie Osmond, Edition 750*

h. Adora Montana Belle, 2002, *Sculpted by Marie Osmond, Edition 1,500*

160

a

a. Adora Beach Belle, 2005, *Sculpted by Marie Osmond, Edition 600*
b. Adora Belle Minnie Me, 2004, *Sculpted by Marie Osmond, Edition 1,000*
c. Adora Belle & Beau Mouseketeers, 2003, *Sculpted by Marie Osmond, Edition 3,000*
d. Mickey & Minnie Wedding Bitty Belles, 2004, *Sculpted by Marie Osmond, Edition 1,500*
e. Adora Belle Disney's Animal Kingdom Tour Guide, 2003, *Sculpted by Marie Osmond, Edition 500*
f. Adora Belle Disney MGM Studios Tour Guide, 2003, *Sculpted by Marie Osmond, Edition 500*
g. Adora Belle Epcot Tour Guide, 2003, *Sculpted by Marie Osmond, Edition 500*
h. Adora Belle Magic Kingdom Tour Guide, 2003, *Sculpted by Marie Osmond, Edition 500*

ADORA *Belle*

b

c

d

e-h

162

a

b

c

d

e

f

a. Adora Belle Disney Store Pin Trader, *2002*
   Sculpted by Marie Osmond, Edition 1,000

b. Adora Belle Tiki Room Pin Trader, *2003*
   Sculpted by Marie Osmond, Edition 1,000

c. Adora Beau Disney Store Pin Trader, *2002*
   Sculpted by Marie Osmond, Edition 1,000

d. Adora Belle & Beau Mouseketeer, *2002*
   Sculpted by Marie Osmond, Edition 300

e. Adora Beau Canoe Pin Trader, *2004*
   Sculpted by Marie Osmond, Edition 1,000

f. Adora Belle-Pirates of the Carribean Pin Trader, *2003*
   Sculpted by Marie Osmond, Edition 1,000

g.

h.

i.

j.

k.

ADORA
Belle

g. The Twilight Zone Tower of Terror™ Adora Belle Pin Trader, 2004, *Sculpted by Marie Osmond, Edition 1,000*

h. Adora Belle Gondolier Hostess, 2002, *Sculpted by Marie Osmond, Edition 1,000*

i. Adora Belle Stitch Fanatic Pin Trader, 2005, *Sculpted by Marie Osmond, Edition 1,000*

*j. Adora Belle Disneyland® Haunted Mansion Hostess, 2002, *Sculpted by Marie Osmond, Edition 1,000*

*k. Adora Belle Eeyore Trick or Treat Pin Trader, 2005, *Sculpted by Marie Osmond, Edition 500*

Not Shown Adora Belle Stitch Trick or Treat Pin Trader, 2005, *Sculpted by Marie Osmond, Edition 500*

*Collectible trading pins not shown

a

a. Adora Minnie Holiday Belle, 2003
  Sculpted by Marie Osmond, Open Edition
b. Adora Belle Disneyland Tour Guide, 2001
  Sculpted by Marie Osmond, Edition 1,000
c. Adora Belle Holiday Pin Trader, 2004
  Sculpted by Marie Osmond, Edition 1,000
d. Adora Minnie Victorian Holiday Belle, 2004
  Sculpted by Marie Osmond, Edition 1,000

c

b

d

a. Fashion A Belle - Ruby, 2004
   Sculpted by Marie Osmond, Edition 500

b. Fashion A Belle - Emerald, 2005
   Sculpted by Marie Osmond, Open Edition

c. Fashion A Belle - Sapphire, 2004
   Sculpted by Marie Osmond, Open Edition

d. Adora Belle Hollywood Star, 2004
   Sculpted by Marie Osmond, Edition 2,232

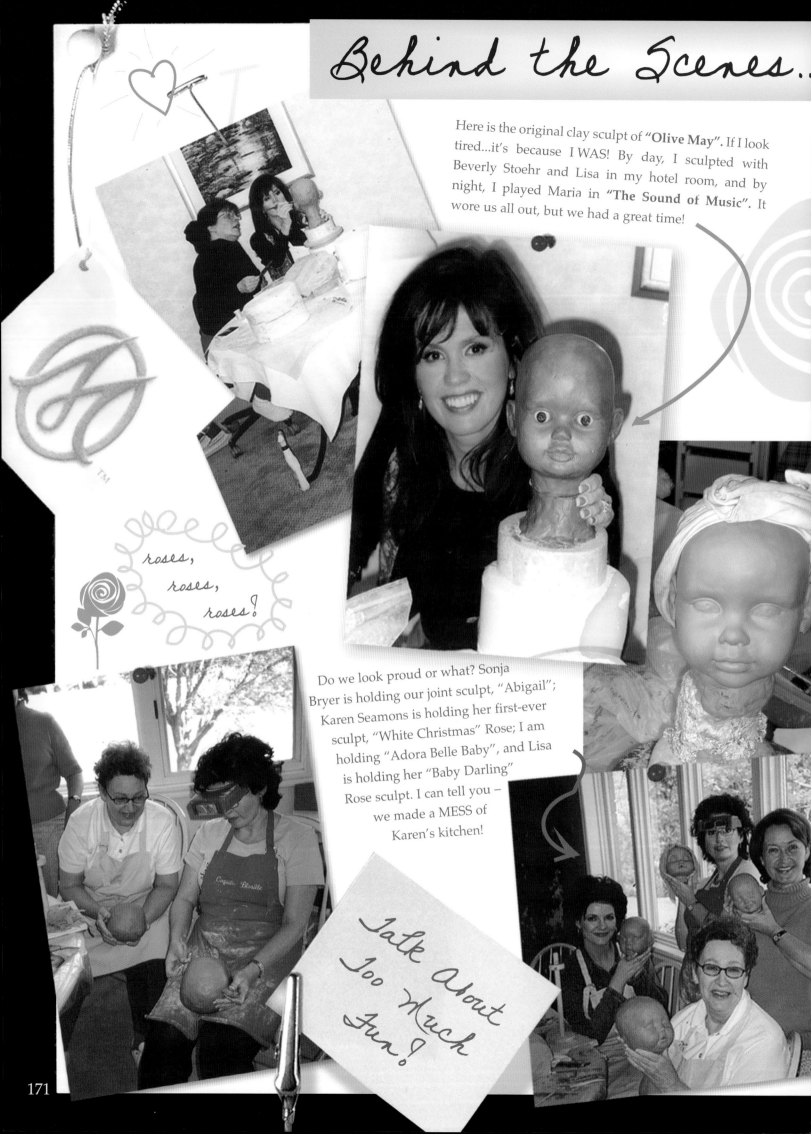

Here is the original clay sculpt of **"Olive May"**. If I look tired...it's because I WAS! By day, I sculpted with Beverly Stoehr and Lisa in my hotel room, and by night, I played Maria in **"The Sound of Music"**. It wore us all out, but we had a great time!

roses, roses, roses!

Do we look proud or what? Sonja Bryer is holding our joint sculpt, "Abigail"; Karen Seamons is holding her first-ever sculpt, "White Christmas" Rose; I am holding "Adora Belle Baby", and Lisa is holding her "Baby Darling" Rose sculpt. I can tell you – we made a MESS of Karen's kitchen!

Talk About Too Much Fun!

Sculpting

My **brother Jimmy** (who is very creative!) stops by to have some sculpting fun. We were sculpting with Karen Scott in my home office. (You know, the one that burned down?!)

Yikes?!

There are two different stories behind this photo depending on **who you believe...** me or Lisa! I claim that I was just trying to help when I pointed out (by digging her doll's eye out of it's head!) that her eyes were uneven. Lisa claims that I destroyed her sculpt and that I should be banned from knives! (She also hasn't let me touch one of her sculpts since!)

13th Rose!

Lisa and I working hard to get this sculpt just right!

Abigail "helping" Mommy as I sculpt "Friendship."

I love Sculpting!

Behind the Scenes...Signings

Me with Mr. & Mrs. Robert Bettle, the proud owners of "The One and Only Cinderella."

Does anyone have a Sharpie?

This photo represents one of my favorite signing moments. The 3 friends surrounding me were strangers to this young girl and her mother as they stood together in line. After seeing their Hershey Kisses dolls, the girl quietly expressed to her mother that she'd love to have this doll. Hearing this, these three "angels" pooled their money and purchased the doll for their new, young friend. I love doll collectors!

Here I pose with "The 3 Maries" at a signing. There's "mother" (in the wheel chair), and her two daughters – and they all share the name, "Marie." I guess then, this makes "The 4 Maries"!

A few of our star retailers, (above left) Allen Rogers with members of my doll team, Tracy Stobaugh and Corrie Hicks; and (above right) Diane Pettinelli and Maria Brady with me.

My longtime Disney pin trading friends.

It was "Father / Daughter Day" at this signing, when Earl Glover and his daughter, Debbie Smoak, pose with my daddy and me.

No end in sight!!

Behind the Scenes...

Friend and colleage, Gary Lowenthal of Boyds Bears, brings "goofing around" on the set at QVC to a whole new level! You just never know what he'll do next (which is why I like him so much!) Here we are with our Quite-a-Pair collaboration, "Beary Best Friends".

Celebrating a Sell-Out Show!

In 1999, we debuted our vinyl "Beauty Bug Ball" dolls on QVC. Lisa, Tammy Knickerbocker, Marie D'Amore and myself costumed each of our daughters as one of the bugs and we had a "Beauty Bug" fashion show on air. It was hysterical! Here is Lisa with her daughter, Alexis, Mary Beth and I.

Christopher Radko and I admire "Adora Belle Radko Ornament", from 1998, on the set of QVC.

175

at QVC

The actual program guide from our first show!

Program Guide - July 29 - Aug 25

JULY 29 - AUGUST 4, 1991

When Mary Beth and I come together on stage for our doll shows, we really do have a lot of fun. It's like two girlfriends getting together to chat about something they both love...Dolls!

My "A" Team...

Lisa, Peggy, me, Connie, Rae and Mary Beth

Lisa and I celebrated 20 years working together in May, 2005. (We were both in grade school when we started!) Here we are in December, 1993, on the set of QVC, getting ready for our holiday show.

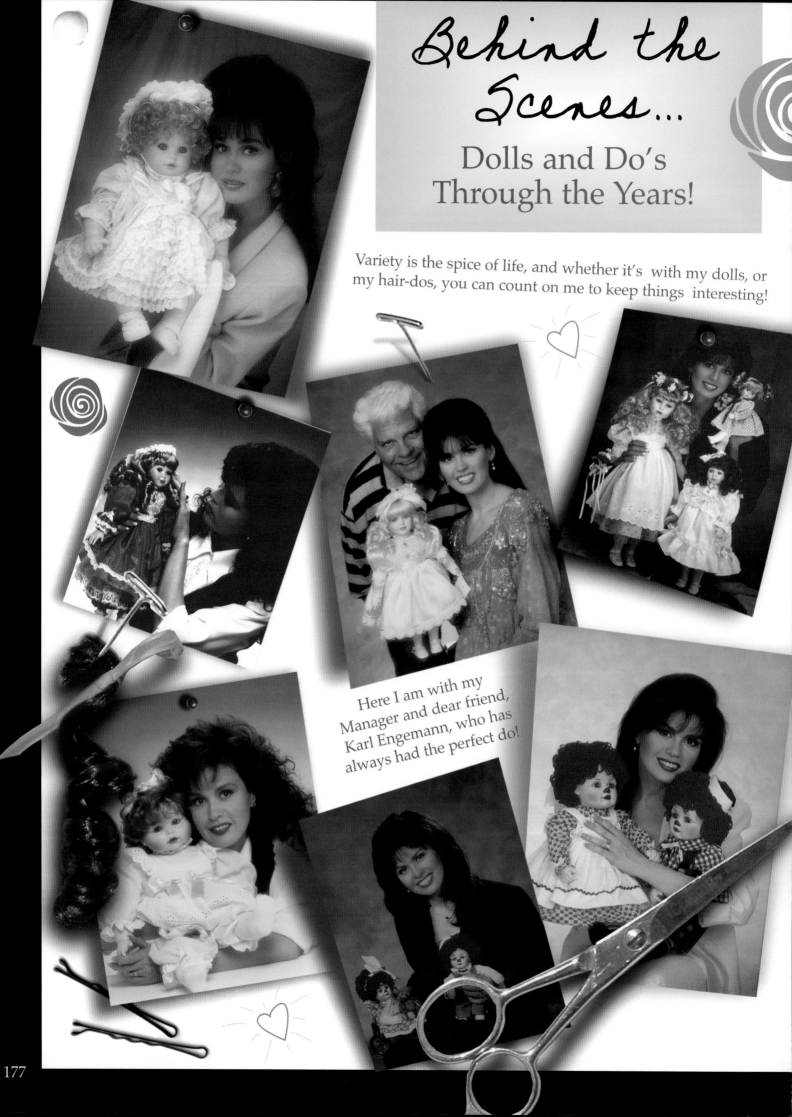

Behind the Scenes...

Dolls and Do's Through the Years!

Variety is the spice of life, and whether it's with my dolls, or my hair-dos, you can count on me to keep things interesting!

Here I am with my Manager and dear friend, Karl Engemann, who has always had the perfect do!

"Oh My!"

(What was I thinking on some of these hairstyles?!)

Hair Do!

Hair Don't!

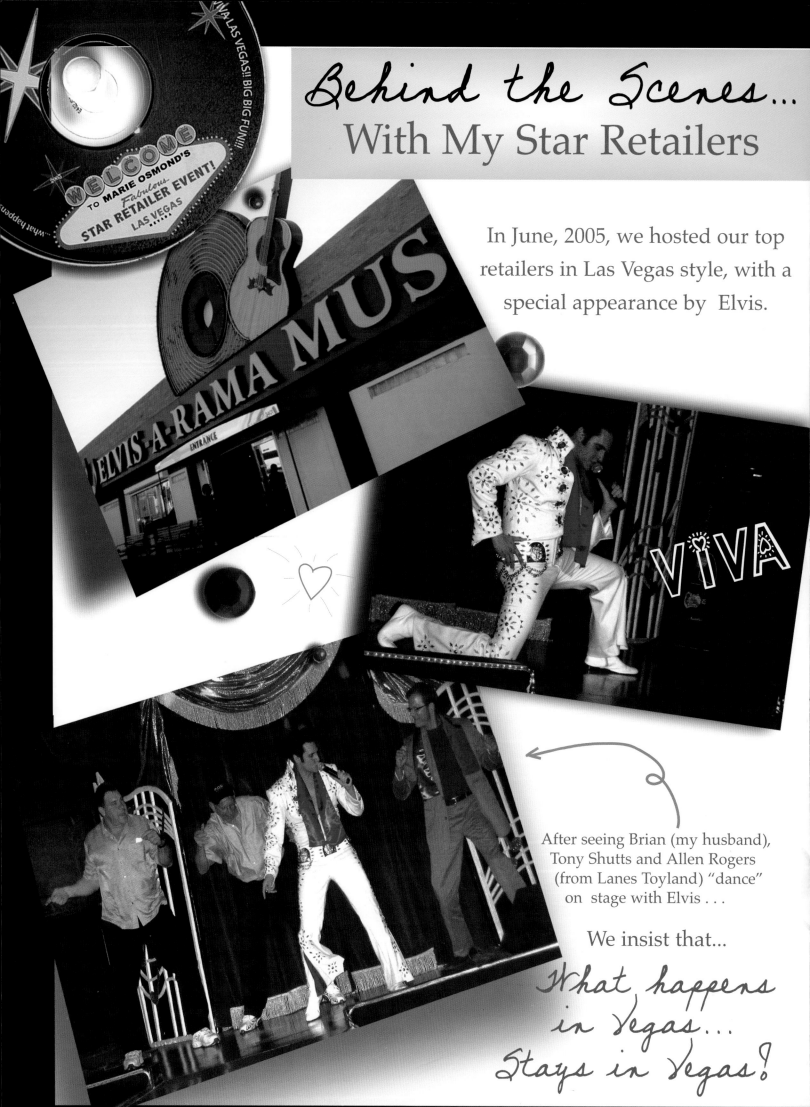

Behind the Scenes...
With My Star Retailers

WELCOME TO MARIE OSMOND'S *Fabulous* STAR RETAILER EVENT! LAS VEGAS

In June, 2005, we hosted our top retailers in Las Vegas style, with a special appearance by Elvis.

VIVA

After seeing Brian (my husband), Tony Shutts and Allen Rogers (from Lanes Toyland) "dance" on stage with Elvis . . .

We insist that...

What happens in Vegas... Stays in Vegas!

LAS VEGAS!

"Elvis has left the pick up!" A box with a few remaining "Elvis" dolls flew off the truck in the middle of the desert on the drive home from Vegas. Jackie Parfitt, Tracy Stobaugh, Corrie Hicks and Michelle Hankins had to tie him down – as he was "all shook up"!

WELCOME
TO MARIE OSMOND'S
Fabulous
STAR RETAILER EVENT
LAS VEGAS
NEVADA

180

Behind the Scenes...
With My Friends

MARIE OSMOND DOLLS

Above, the Marie Doll Friends
gather for their annual reunion.
Then we have (right and clockwise)
Daddy/Daughter date; Peggy, me
and Lisa; me with Lily and John Chen
and finally, my dear friend, Kesti Poulsen.

It's a girlfriend thing!

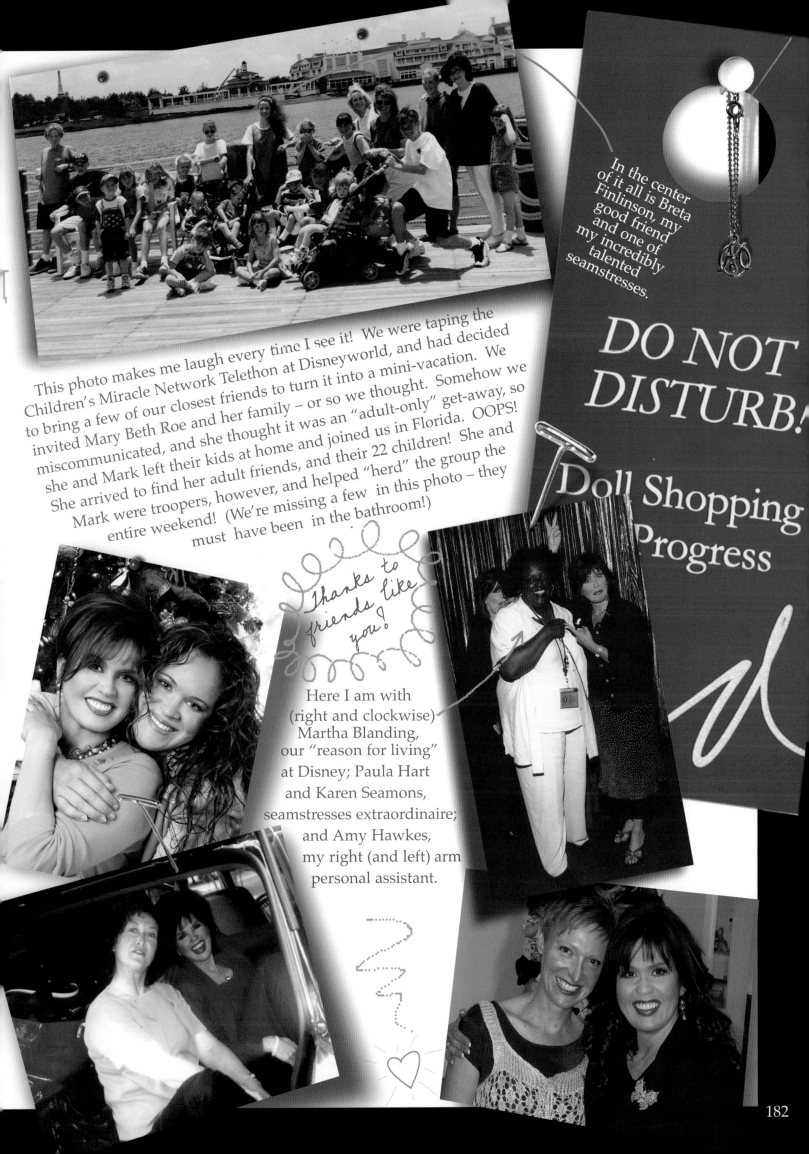

This photo makes me laugh every time I see it! We were taping the Children's Miracle Network Telethon at Disneyworld, and had decided to bring a few of our closest friends to turn it into a mini-vacation. We invited Mary Beth Roe and her family – or so we thought. Somehow we miscommunicated, and she thought it was an "adult-only" get-away, so she and Mark left their kids at home and joined us in Florida. OOPS! She arrived to find her adult friends, and their 22 children! She and Mark were troopers, however, and helped "herd" the group the entire weekend! (We're missing a few in this photo – they must have been in the bathroom!)

In the center of it all is Breta Finlinson, my good friend and one of my incredibly talented seamstresses.

DO NOT DISTURB!

Doll Shopping Progress

Thanks to friends like you!

Here I am with (right and clockwise) Martha Blanding, our "reason for living" at Disney; Paula Hart and Karen Seamons, seamstresses extraordinaire; and Amy Hawkes, my right (and left) arm personal assistant.

Artist Biographies

Mary Benner

When Mary Benner was a little girl, she loved playing with dolls. Her grandmother loved dolls too, and when Mary visited her on the farm, she had full access to the huge trunk in the attic that was filled with old dolls, doll clothing and accessories.

As Mary grew up, her love of dolls was put "on hold". Then in 1989, her passion was revived when she attended a doll making class with a friend. The rest, as they say, is history. With encouragement from her husband, Mary's doll business grew and thrived, and then in 1996, Mary added a new dimension when she began sculpting her own artist dolls. Mary specializes in elegantly detailed Victorian era costuming for her artist dolls and her beloved antique re-creations. An award winning artist, Mary and her husband, Allen (her right-hand man!), have two daughters.

Sonja Bryer

Sonja Bryer has loved dolls all of her life. Her home and studio are an impressive "museum" of the many dolls she's sculpted and collected through the years.

1980 was a benchmark year for Sonja as she began selling her dolls commercially; became a member of ODACA and UFDC doll associations; and won several (of what would become many) awards for her first portrait doll.

Since that time, she has received many other honors, including having her sculpt, "Norma Jean," featured on the cover of "Contemporary Doll" magazine. Sonja's sculpts have a uniquely feminine distinction to them. She is truly a master portrait sculptor.

Penelope Carr

As a child, Penelope Carr loved making mud and papier-mâché sculpture, and still loves working in water-based clay. Even as a single parent, Penelope managed to do her art: apple doll caricatures, soft sculptures, and custom clothing design and construction.

When Penelope purchases gifts for others, they are almost always art supplies. Her home became a studio for neighborhood kids. Says Penelope, "The joy in a child's face after creating something is truly beautiful, and that delight in learning permeates my life and work."

An award-winning sculptor and painter, Penelope is still drawn to sculpting delighted, mischievous, innocent, loving infants and toddlers which comes from a special, bubbly place in her soul!

Michael Evert

After studying in Pittsburgh and Rome, Italy, Michael Evert moved to New York City in 1981 and began wide-ranging work as a sculptor. He has done the original sculpture for many mannequins, including projects for the Costume Institute of the Metropolitan Museum of Art, working from life with prominent fashion models as well as with illustrators and fashion designers. His first doll sculpt was Mel Odom's Gene in 1992 and he has done a number of dolls with Mel, Marie and others since. He lives in downtown Manhattan with his wife, son, and daughter who are all presently coping with a new puppy.

Breta Finlinson

Breta Finlinson has been designing and sewing doll costumes since she was a young girl. She and her cousin, Jeni, would spend hours meticulously hand sewing clothing for their tiniest dolls, some only one inch tall.

In high school she worked as a seamstress at the Osmond Studio Costume Shop in Orem, Utah. And at age 17 she began touring with the Osmond Family as their wardrobe mistress.

In 1993, while expecting her 5th child, she designed her first doll for Marie's collectible doll line. She continues to enjoy "playing" dolls and is especially fond of designing costumes for Marie's smallest dolls.

Emily Garthright

Emily Garthright is an artist, painter and seamstress. She began sculpting in 1997, and has since won almost every doll award there is! When it comes to dolls, she envisions herself as a "simple storyteller".

Emily traces her love for storytelling to her childhood in Tennessee, where growing up as an only child, she used her creative imagination often. While her little friends were making mud pies, Emily made "mud dolls" and accessorized them with bird feathers, grass and multicolored leaves.

Emily credits her mother for teaching her the value of "doing it right or not doing it at all". Emily is a perfectionist to this day and follows her heart in her sculpts and designs.

Joke Grobben

Joke was born in 1945 in The Hague, Netherlands. A student of sculpture in both The Hague and Florence, Italy, Joke was asked to sculpt a portrait of a friend's child. This launched her career as a doll artist. Joke's dolls inspire both collectors and doll artists everywhere. For Joke, making doll-children of the world is her island refuge in the sea.

Paula Nelson-Hart

Paula Nelson-Hart, a self proclaimed creative diva, lives, works and creates "outside the box." She grew up in Southern California, where her mother filled her childhood with a passion for art, design and creativity, lovingly supporting Paula's early clothing design efforts by allowing her to wear some of those first (and often very odd) creations to grade school. Paula studied fashion design at the Fashion Institute of Design and Merchandising in Los Angeles, and then continued her education at Brigham Young University. Living in the mountains near Sundance, Utah, she loves to integrate her love of nature and the inspiration of "her mountain" in her designs. "I love the challenge of translating nature's perfection into wearable art, especially for these beautiful dolls," exclaims Paula.

Linda Henry-Boving

Linda Henry-Boving began her doll sculpting career in 1980, studying with such famous doll artists as Lee Middleton and Faith Wick, and in 1987, she began designing her own original mohair teddy bears, as well.

In 1990, Linda began sculpting for the Marie Osmond Doll brand, making her one of the first artists to sculpt for Marie's collection. Additionally, during her career, Linda has designed for several other manufacturers, including Lee Middleton Original Dolls, L.L. Knickerbocker Creations, the Annette Funicello Bear Collection, and the Georgetown Collection.

Linda is an award-winning doll and bear artist who has traveled extensively exhibiting her works of art.

Shirley Hunter-Peck

Shirley Hunter Peck was born in the 1940's – before T.V., so she learned to sew at the young age of 8, making dolly clothes. One of her favorite things to do was make paper dolls out of the Sears catalogue – complete with appliances and furniture cut and pasted on cardboard walls. (Play required a lot of imagination then!)

In 1984, Shirley's love of fabric, dolls and art turned into something that encompassed it all . . . doll making, specializing in dolls that are completely made of wool felt.

Careful attention to detail and quality materials are worked into every aspect of Shirley's designs from the costuming to each charming face, creating works of art that will become heirlooms to treasure.

Ping Lau

Ping Lau was raised and educated in Singapore. She graduated with a Bachelor of Arts in English Literature from the National University of Singapore. She returned to her "true calling" in art, however, after immigrating to the United States in 1989.

Although she has been painting all of her life, she began sculpting dolls in earnest when she came to America and realized how many people shared her fascination and love of dolls. Her dolls are meticulously detailed, depicting children of all ethnic groups, which reflect her own exposure to many different cultures throughout the world.

Her dolls receive tremendous response and recognition and are occasionally mistaken for real children!

Tawny Nix

Tawny Nix comes from a family of talented artisans. Sewing, crocheting, knitting and making crafts has been passed down through the generations of her family, so crafting comes naturally to her.

When she first started making dolls, they were primitive cloth dolls. She loved the feel of the cloth dolls, but wanted more depth in their faces. Tawny read an article about molding cloth over a sculpted medium, and hence, a lot of experimenting and designing began.

She started with molding a dyed fabric over other artist's porcelain heads, but she desired to use her own faces, so she taught herself how to sculpt from books and also how to create her own molds. "I can't tell you how many plaster disasters I've had in my garage", says Tawny! In 1998, her hobby turned into a part-time business, as she started selling her original dolls at area craft and doll shows.

Tawny is an award-winning artist who says, "I feel very blessed to have been given the opportunity to share my talents and give something that evokes emotion in people . . . happiness, comfort and joy. For me, that is the best thing about being a doll artist."

Jo Ann Pohlman

Jo Ann Pohlman lives in a suburb of Chicago, where for many years she worked from her home, teaching ceramics and doll making classes, specializing in reproduction dolls.

After spending several years working with others' sculpts, she felt a desire and need to start sculpting her own originals. She is a self-taught artist who began sculpting dolls in the mid-1990's. Jo Ann has sculpted dolls for many of the industry's top companies. She has a unique ability to capture the innocence and realism of a child.

Jo Ann is inspired by the expressions and personalities of small children and it is her desire that collectors enjoy her dolls as much as she enjoys creating them!

Cheryl Robinson

From bowling balls to porcelain dolls, Cheryl Robinson has had her hands full. Prior to making dolls, Cheryl was a professional bowler for 15 years. She began making dolls in 1985 with her mother-in-law, which helped fill a void left in both of their lives from the loss of a loved one. Cheryl describes making dolls as "a blessing in disguise". After nine years of making dolls on her own, Cheryl joined the L.L. Knickerbocker team in 1995, crafting several reproduction dolls for Marie's line including Lauren, Grandma Kit, Morgan, and Charlotte, (one of Cheryl's favorite dolls). She and her husband, Jay, have two daughters, Leahna and Lauren.

Karen Scott

Karen began sculpting porcelain dolls in 1989 when her mother read an article about doll sculpting. Knowing her daughter's artistic ability, Karen's mother went out and purchased some clay and sculpting supplies, dumped the lot on a table in front of Karen and told her to get started. The rest is history!

Karen enjoys sculpting all types of dolls, and reveals that "when I am truly into a work, something else seems to take over, so that my hands seem almost to work of themselves."

Karen not only credits her mother with her love and talent for doll making, but her father as well. He is an accomplished portrait artist, and Karen was following in his footsteps until the sculpting bug bit her. "Once I stuck my fingers into the clay, I was hooked," says Karen. "And I haven't drawn another portrait since!"

Karen Seamons

Karen began her costume designing when, at the age of six, she created costumes for tag board paper dolls.

She jumped into sewing for profit one Christmas season, designing an entire Barbie fashion show for her sister Michele; her friends; and their moms, grossing a whopping $10!

Karen loved designing and sewing her own clothes as well, and she received her B.S. Degree from Brigham Young University in Clothing Construction and Textiles. Time would prove the wisdom of this decision, as she was able to combine being a stay-at-home mom with a career she enjoyed. (She and her husband, Ron, have 6 children.)

Although Karen has created her own clothing line for Nordstrom; had her own sewing business; does film work, including "Touched By An Angel" to name a few . . . working with the Marie brand, Karen admits she's come full circle, back to the very thing she began doing as a young girl, designing and sewing for dolls. "Working with Marie and Lisa, is the best way I could use my talents. I love doing this, and the three of us have become good friends along the way!"

Beverly Stoehr

First ceramics; then reproduction dolls; then ultimately being tutored by Hummel's Master Sculptor . . . Beverly Stoehr finally began sculpting her own dolls in 1989, which she admits, "Was the beginning of a new life for me."

Beverly met Marie Osmond in 1997. They formed a successful working relationship and a treasured friendship, resulting in many collaborations together, including Marie's first real sculpting effort . . . "Olive May".

Beverly enjoys teaching other budding sculptors as well, as they develop their skills to create treasures for future doll collectors. She is an award-winning sculptor who offers this sage advice based on personal experience . . . "If you have a dream or passion for something, don't be afraid to follow it. Sometimes, those dreams come true!"

Additional
Artists

Jessica Antoinette

Ralph Bienert

Carole Bowling

Adrienne Brown

Berdine Creedy

Caroli Gardiner

Joann Gelin

Maryse Nicole

Nelda Pieper

Debbie Sampson

Rita Schmidt

Susan Scogin

Kathy Smith-Fitzpatrick

Biographies not available

For in-depth biographies of these and other artists, please visit our website:
marieosmond.com

Index

By Doll Name

continued

Index

By Collection

continued

MARIE OSMOND
DOLLS

15th

"FRIENDS LIKE YOU"

ANNIVERSARY
1991-2006

Thank You!

I was taught early on that the defining mark of a great doll is in the details. However, I've come to understand in these past 15 years that the defining mark of a great doll line is in the dedication of all those who pay attention to the details.

I have had the privilege of creating with, and for, people whose high standards daily challenge and invigorate me to make every Marie Osmond doll the *best* it can be…every tiny detail.

My gratitude goes out to the **gifted artists**: sculptors, designers and seamstresses who constantly astonish and delight me, and to Lily Chen and her hard-working team.

To the **doll retailers**, for their loyalty to collectible dolls and the loving care they give their customers.

To **bj Pergola** at Charisma, for the marathon hours she spent on the photography and the graphic design to make this book come together so gracefully.

To my **QVC partners**, who were the first to believe that I was both passionate and knowlegable about dolls. They gave me the first venue in which to share my doll line with millions of collectors.

My limitless appreciation to those who have given me continuous support and who understand and exceed my expectations of quality:

Karl Engemann: My Manager and my second dad, who's been with me, making it all happen in the best and most fun way, ever since Mattel made me into a 24-inch modeling doll!

Kesti Poulsen: My Marie Osmond Dolls Web Site Manager. Her infectious enthusiasm has made her a favorite with my collectors and someone I hope I never have to do without.

Amy Hawkes: Our vigilant Executive Assistant for Marie, Inc. She keeps all of the ducks in a row, even on those days we are all running around her like chickens with our heads cut off! She's the best.

Marcia Wilkie: Who takes the thoughts from my head, blends it so well with the intention of my heart, and spins my dyslexic words into sense for each of my books, articles, and speeches. You without it couldn't I, Marsh….whoops, I mean…I couldn't do it without you, Marsh!

Peggy Vicioso: Our exceptional Vice President of Marketing and Product Development for Charisma, a true "go for it" and "go for it all" girlfriend. A stellar arm of my "A Team" triangle.

Tony Shutts, Marty Krasner, and every Charisma Brands employee that works so hard to make Marie Osmond Dolls the *best* dolls on the planet!

And endless thanks and love to **Lisa Hatch**, my brilliant Creative Director of Marie, Inc. She is truly my twin traveler in this sometimes exhausting, but mostly exhilirating adventure called life. She continues to bring daily steadfast friendship, incredible foresight and fresh ideas into each of these fifteen years. She is definitely the right arm of the "A Team".

Last , but not least, all my love and appreciation to **my husband, Brian Blosil**: who re-energized my doll business through his insight and ingenuity and made it possible to continue producing my doll line. He has made all of my dreams come true.

Finally, my sincere gratitude to the real reason I design dolls: YOU! I find profound joy in sharing your passion for collecting, the sincere community of caring collectors, and most of all . . . your delight in the details!

My Doll Friends and Memories

emy donald bella wyatt zachary sophia marcus eric jason sheila troy heather andelyn aspen brittney shane justin ma
v max michael alex tiffany doug tyler nathan sarah zachary carson braydon maria paula wendy david martha laralee r
ni alan josh adam gerri wendy cheryl tina christopher mark hayley beth darlene mary beth rae emily marty tony kare
yne mr. chen cody winnie leo sherry rex mr. wong peggy penny debra connie karen kesti amy marcia allen steve lis
nmy wendy justin bobby kylie kendall becky lisa bill dotty mellissa chad haley harrison sandra kate liz jason luke a
na donna tamera ron iris gerri nancee sharla eric kayla michell steve martina neva lyndsay norman gaynelle jimmy t
atthew zoila desiree tamra marianne celeste lora kimber india martin rosa trudy melinda meg lynette rena glynda shi
rian alonna dolly harriet penney angelina terriann maryrose jaye reyna lynnette fatima eda oreanna daveen ruth jam
th marina julianne patrica deeya char lorilee glenda lou ann evelyn michele jeri jo abigail velma anthony anthea sta
helle maryellen mandi fonda tania adrienne beth denyce nanc franz anamaria jodie lorre antonina marcella cary anet
ave cecilia lyn grettie tamala greta johnna gailen len daniel derryle shelley lynn dieu-kim kassandra gaye bernardett
ck loree monique michael jean bette joana trisha letty doreen maude pauline ray rick joy shaun britany megan kimb
ida cyndi laurene davetta rolanda andrea kaitlyn karl judy cristine georgi ana dotty emilie caress lee jaimi owl suzan
a bernice sephie bob dora jann aleta erin shellie danitza sun kelli barbara marylynn caitlyn joanie charlotte gigi jeff jh
nna marie kris vickey kathie amy eloise renea colleen gregg pat teremarie drema adeline sally ingrid colette rob she
am gerald eileen reta susanna arjayra jonna george nathalie suchesne trientje therese cheri rosemary geraldine kimber
argaret dusty elaine gail fillisha pansy paulie vesta virgil jinafer marie kiriaki lynda jandi paulette mitch deeann lise
eilah lucy olivia angie miss billie jacqueline hanne bev dorthy sara noka maria beatrice mickey arils jayna darci sherle
rro tamie evie rejane bessie hope rochelle jeanine mary nn melva christine tammya edwina susie alberta toni cindy alb
rnadette sonja ada becki kiley geneva shehnaz jukie karin colleen nonda katey leda shellegh dina marie fredda pia r
nielle sharyn desirae lauire sylvia roxanne leta dawn shalawn sandi mei mei sharron sueanne cathi arleen dina teah k
nna tish gailee kimberleeloren jan helle kristin leann verona cassandra normalou gwenyth jennette carrie ann tammi k
arin manolya randy tina ray claire ginny sandra nacho leannette dianne alex sissy morgan george anna beverly mia l
urdes trina enid lorais di tara ronnie lowana chris lita shey mavis nadine karrie marlin vanessa lila genese rosana sta
setta joellen reanee imelda debra mariann barry ross jordyn holly caitilin patricia shirley jacklynn melany elsbeth matt
ean brenda sher lea jennilyn maricela dezeraye katarina rachelle christine charlsa lawanna tressia andria amber sharr
rol renee teri marggy su gayle mercy neita juanita dee ruby sherry barbaraj shane olwen vickie emma jenni cami delore
lie mallory sabina anne palma amie georganna brianna zoe gena darilyn janey jason jenny maryln ginger velita robin
zanne tanya yvette shay kerri thomas carmen doris marguerite ruth ann emily rita marielba peggy bernadine brian a
lie ken roy douglas kitsa flo jenessa noel angi camille deb shelly ramona layna marjean tamarah penny shelby frank
onda mercedes joella cierra kristie carolanne jonda fuzzy jolie regina jacque shari darlene bethania cathy cathleen lin
osa cortes collin sadie monica sarah lily nancy helena roxanna elva ernestine mela mariana nora danna connie lesliar
xie jennifer casi nataleah jolly willa gaileen libby gina brigitte patty scott esther stannah coby kaylene belva carolmari
n ethel mischelle melea traci mary jane kavitha johna cordelia kara lili delila benita micki jolea antoinette manette ales
artha rhona venus iva jenifer mel marta tuya dawnmarie alta claudine tillie teresa varan andre'a florence leigh tammy
nni ronald nanci dorothy rosalie annelise tasha lana nicki betheny janine ladonna lu anne savannah frannie jolynn m.
e larry nelma karon christiane aicel margarita conie melonie sherri jane paul alisha romelle jose ciney jenise dawnah
cialena dara barbra wonyoung marjorie vivian debby lin rose marie lorna trudi katrina gen dottie alison camilia frankl
elodee judi adella amelia cynthis helene veronica carly jackie anna maggie ronda alicia gladys kathryne kristina gise
nny sherri nicola felice ursula wanda brona helen felicity concetta shirle polly sheree lynne joann jaci jerrilynn hilda c
ni merry nenita whitney nayda elishia gwen erna winifred delma vicki mary anne betty violet louise roxann sherre j
n terri erlinda dolores caroline denise celina june caren chelsea patrick gene gerber maxine teena christie shauna and
ida winnie jill gloria sabrina lillian fay rosalia jerry yolanda camilla tana fransje mindy babs natalia geri william farah
mberli paula sondra adeana jeanne blanca loryn micky päivi ilia lisa rachael konnie matthew antonia bill carrie meag
n elise tracey leslie nell ileana romelia katie dana marie summer caryn tiffany gioiella mariane alene donan ann marie
rde fern eitrt laren deon deanna patrice justine donni daphne kelsie evalani peri hilary maylene claudia tamara jeanni
dine fidelina ann karyn joleen kelley lucinda rhonnie mitzi mary suzanne kandilyn kathy chris jimmy donny wayne jay
ianna brandon michael rachael jessica stephen brian augey ginny paul scott scout joani katrina joey mike betty orlan
naomi sheryl leon roseanne beverly jill leslie natalie john vicki cyndi reenie nancy joy mary suzanne kathy chris jim
ephen brian augey warren krystal rebecca ginny joani katrina joey mike betty orlando cheri tim jean tammy wendy jus
ia aj naomi sheryl leon roseanne beverly jill leslie jimmy donnycara sharon rhonda mercedes joella cierra kristie caro
aron gay-maree kaydra romona nelda olga leah betty ann tonda isabel ed diosa cortes collin sadie monica sarah lily
y norton herlide sandy logan mary lillianna nina heather timothy lindsey dixie jennifer casi nataleah jolly willa gailee
ura lesley elisabeth sari sonya freddie audra mary jo pandy frances eva em ethel mischelle melea traci mary jane kavi